REACHING HIGH:

The Psychology of Spiritual Living

Marvin Gawryn

REACHING HIGH:

The Psychology of Spiritual Living

Spiritual Renaissance Press
Berkeley, California

REACHING HIGH:
The Psychology of Spiritual Living

Copyright © 1980 Marvin Gawryn
Cover design by
Rebecca Marshall and Martha Bredemeyer

Published by: SPIRITUAL RENAISSANCE PRESS

315 Harvard Ln.
Boulder, CO
80302

ISBN 0-938380-00-1 Hardcover
ISBN 0-938380-01-X Softcover

Library of Congress Catalog Card Number: 80-24306
Library of Congress Cataloging in Publication Data:
Gawryn, Marvin, 1951–
Reaching High:
The Psychology of Spiritual Living
1. Spiritual life. 2. Psychology, Religious.
I. Title.
BL624.G37   291.4'48   80-24306

First Edition
2 3 4 5 6 7 8 9

Printed in the United States of America

DEDICATION

*To all those who ask the ultimate questions,
and begin the search.*

MARVIN GAWRYN received his B.A. degree from Antioch College in Yellow Springs, Ohio. He completed his studies in psychology with a Master's degree from the Graduate School of Human Behavior at United States International University in San Diego, California. He has taught at University of California, San Diego, and Armstrong College in Berkeley, California. He is registered with the California State Board of Behavioral Science Examiners as a Marriage, Family, and Child Counselor.

Mr. Gawryn is the Director of Highreach Services in Berkeley, California. He also works with the Clinic for Adults and Children in San Leandro, which provides therapy for individuals, couples, and families.

Mr. Gawryn has long been concerned with how living spiritually can lead people to overall psychological health and happiness. He has written extensively on the psychology of spiritual living and has conducted seminars on this topic for groups all around the United States and Canada.

Mr. Gawryn can be contacted through Highreach Services, P.O. Box 427, Berkeley, California, 94701.

Preface

FOR SOME TIME NOW I have had the deep privilege of working as an individual and family therapist. I have intimately shared in the pain and confusion, and the healing and growth of many people. I have had the honor of being invited into the inner lives of my spiritual brothers and sisters, and have enjoyed the awesome opportunity of knowing and loving them.

I have felt people struggle with doubt, fear, and despair. And I have seen the mind-boggling transformations that result when people begin to work in partnership with God.

Many people today are alone and drifting, starving for hope, love, and a vision by which to live. The tragedy is that the vision they seek, the way of living they so desperately crave, exists within and around them if they will only open their eyes to see it. A life of fulfillment and purpose is within their immediate grasp, if they will but reach for it.

In writing this book I have attempted to combine practical psychological insights and powerful spiritual truths into a comprehensive overview of how to live spiritually. I have striven for a clear and vivid description of the deepest of inner experiences.

If you are searching spiritually, if you yearn to know your place and purpose in the grand scheme of things, this book has been written for you. You may be a professional or a laborer, sophisticated or simple, spiritually advanced or just beginning; if you wish to grow spiritually this book will help you do it.

My sincere hope is that many people will reach high for the exhilarating joys of the spiritual life. If through these pages even one single person finds his way to a living relationship with God, this book will have entirely fulfilled its purpose.

Berkeley, California   M.G.
1980

ACKNOWLEDGEMENTS

Numerous people deserve thanks for their help in the production of this book. They include Vern Bennom Grimsley, Dr. Jeff Wattles, Joy Wattles, David Gray, Daniel Dickinson, Craig Buck, Dr. Roland Tapp, David Kantor, Martha Bredemeyer, and Rebecca Marshall. Special thanks go to my wife, Francyl, my parents, Leon and Pearl, and my sister, Myrna, for their warm encouragement throughout the long months of manuscript preparation.

CONTENTS

ix

PART III

VIEWPOINTS: THE PERSONALITY'S PERSPECTIVE

PART IV

SPIRITUAL LIVING: THE DYNAMIC PERSONALITY

Introduction

L ET US BEGIN with a few very basic questions:

A trillion star-suns shine in the night sky. Why?
Four billion people live on our world. What are we doing here?
We exist. We think. We feel. For what purpose?
What is man? What is his place in the universe?
Days, months, years are passing. Where are we going?
How can a person find real fulfillment and peace?

The earliest of men yearned for answers to such questions. Modern men and women find themselves returning to these same musings. And future generations without end will carry on the search; for the urge to find the answers to such ultimate questions is rooted in the very deepest parts of human personality.

PART I OF THIS BOOK addresses the question, "What is human personality?" Before considering man's place in reality we must first understand what man himself is: the body which sees and touches; the mind which thinks thoughts and feels emotions; the soul which senses truth, beauty, goodness, and love; and the inner Spirit which so devotedly leads us forward. And at the core lies the human will, the ship's captain of personality, choosing, deciding, acting, and determining the course of life. These parts all become balanced and integrated within the unified personality.

1

FROM AN UNDERSTANDING of the individual personality it is natural to move on to a consideration of relationships between personalities. Relationships are the source of our greatest challenges and our deepest satisfactions. Part II begins with a look at that relationship which is the foundation and ideal for all others, the loving friendship that God has with each human being. Our relations with all the people around us follow naturally from the heart of this guiding inner pattern. Love is the lifeblood of such relationships, and we first learn the ways of love within the circle of the family.

MOVING OUT PAST the near limitless circle of relationships, Part III explores the purposes that underlie all of reality. What part do we play in this vast creation? Is the universe a fearsome or a friendly place? Our view of life and how we fit into it has a tremendous impact on how fulfilled we can be.

PART IV TAKES A CLOSER look at the actual process of spiritual living. Day to day life is a profound school of growth where the goal is not only to *know* and *understand* the truth, but also to *become* it. A person can never become a star athlete by merely believing in exercise; he has to actually exercise. Real religion goes beyond mere belief; it is an actual way of living with God.

THIS BOOK FOCUSES ON the personal spiritual experience of the individual. Each of us who looks for the ultimate answers sets out on a unique inner adventure. If we choose, each of us can embark this very day on a never-ending voyage of spiritual discovery, an eternal quest for the treasures of a personal relationship with God.

THERE IS AN ANCIENT legend which concerns a meeting of the gods dating back well before the beginning of time. They were discussing a hiding place for the Spirit which man would be unable to find. (Why they ever wanted to hide the Spirit in the first place remains a mystery.) Suggestions ranged from the bottom of the ocean to the mountains of the moon, but the gods simply could not feel assured that man would not eventually reach these places and find the Spirit.

At long last (which can last quite long before the beginning of time), a minor deity came up with the brilliant idea of hiding the Spirit within man himself. The gods all congratulated themselves heartily, for certainly that was the one place that man would never think to look.

Well, thankfully, the gods of ancient legends are renowned for their lapses of wisdom. If we are searching spiritually there is indeed one place where we can most certainly find and know God. He waits patiently within us.

PART I

The Sum of the Parts: Unifying Personality

Introduction to Part I

IT WAS AN HISTORIC MOMENT when a primitive half-man crouching fearfully beside a jungle pool first recognized the reflection on the water's shimmering surface as his own. His descendants have continued a long tradition of fascinated self-scrutiny. Few studies have absorbed man as much as the exploration of human nature itself.

The Greeks summed up this trend in a tidy two-word command to the philosophers of the day: Know Thyself. Religion down through the centuries has also contributed offerings to the quest for self-understanding. Modern psychology, in attempting to describe human personality, is the most recent contributor to the search.

There is a reason for our having devoted so much effort to self-exploration. Before embarking on a world cruise, the wise sailor makes sure he knows his vessel. Before considering why we are here or how we can be happy, it is obviously important for us to begin to understand our own nature.

As the search for self-understanding has unfolded, many a powerful thinker has become stranded on the side road of a partial view of human nature. One theorist says man is a complex machine. Another says he is an irrational bundle of emotions. A third is sure he is nothing more than a series of experiences. Still a fourth sees man as a being of wisdom and virtue.

Each of these worthy thinkers claims to have the whole picture, but each actually describes only a small part of the puzzle of personality. What we need is an understanding of all the parts and how they work together to form the whole, the unified personality.

Chapters 1 and 2 briefly describe the four essential parts of personality: body, mind, Spirit, and soul. How can these parts work

7

together in a balanced and unified way? Our human will holds the key to this directive process. Like the conductor of an orchestra, will can weave together the functions of the different parts, coordinating them into the beautiful and effective performance of the whole personality. Chapter 3 takes an in-depth look at this process of will unification.

AN APPLE TREE is not simply a series of fibers and fluids randomly thrown together. Intricate design and the animating force of life bring the separate elements of the tree together into a working whole. Similarly, personality is not simply the random addition of body, mind, Spirit, and soul. Personality is the underlying foundation that brings these parts together into a working whole.

Have you ever seen the insides of an old radio? Each glass tube has its own function. Yet they all plug into a metal plate, called the chassis, which hooks them together in the right way. Similarly, body, mind, Spirit, and soul each fit into the overall pattern of personality. Personality is the medium within which they interact; it hooks them up in the right way. The natural function of personality is to unify itself and the world around it.

Each of our personalities is a complete Self, a complex living pattern of self-identity. Each of our personality patterns is unique; there is none other like it. Regardless of how much we may grow or change, we nevertheless each remain the same unique personality.

Personality is self-conscious. We can look at ourselves and consider our relation to other things around us. And as personalities we can enter into relationships with other personalities.

The most important quality that sets personality apart, the function that is the very essence of personality, is conscious free will. As personalities we can question, choose, decide, and act. We can consciously determine the course of our lives.

BUT FROM WHERE does this priceless personality, this unique identity, come to us? God, who is the author of all reality, is also the originator of human personality. God is Himself the original, infinite, and eternal Personality. It is He who has created and given us our personalities, the very gifts of our selves. In the deepest sense, God is the loving Father of all personalities; thus, each human being is His spiritual child.

CHAPTER

1

The Body/Mind Foundation

THE ROSE IN FULL BLOOM has long been a symbol of beauty and love. However, the deep red blossom does not just magically appear. It is the culmination of the entire root, branch, and leaf structure of the rose bush. Without the feeding and support provided by such a foundation, the rose could not exist.

Similarly, the uppermost blossoming of personality is the spiritual life. But it rests upon the necessary foundation of the physical and mental lives.

Each part of our personalities works within one of these three levels. The body is rooted within physical reality. The mind branches into the mental realm of ideas and meanings. And the Spirit and soul blossom within the spiritual level of ideals, values, and higher truth. A brief examination of the body/mind foundation is important to a full exploration of the higher spiritual life.

THE BODY: BRIDGE BETWEEN TWO WORLDS

The physical body is the bridge which connects our inner and outer worlds. In a sense, it carries two-way traffic. First, it brings the outer world in through the wonder of the physical senses. Second, it enables us to project our inner ideas and visions outward into reality, thereby changing the world around us.

Through its senses, the body can carry inward the splendor of an ocean sunset, the enigma of a melting ice-cube, or the smiling face of a friend. It brings in the raw material of physical experience which is used by the rest of personality.

Using our bodies, we can also transform the outer world in the direction of our inner ideas and values. We can sculpt statues, construct machinery, or express our love through service to other human beings.

Since our bodies serve such a crucial linking function between our inner and outer lives, it is most important that we keep them in the healthiest condition possible. Just like a trusty automobile, in order to provide the most dependable service our bodies must be well maintained. Adequate amounts of sleep, exercise, and proper food contribute to their smooth and vibrant functioning. Extremes of physical indulgence or deprivation disrupt that bodily balance which provides the best foundation for the harmonious working together of the whole personality.

For example, suppose you have not slept for twenty-four hours, have eaten poorly for the last three days, and have been lying around the house smoking, drinking, and taking drugs to calm down, perk up, and inject entertainment into your life. It's likely that you will be mentally and emotionally confused and spiritually despondent. The mind, soul, Spirit and will work together most effectively when the body system is vibrant and well-balanced.

EACH PERSON'S BODY is unique; no other body is quite like it. The structure of our bodies plays a part in our temperaments. Whether we tend to be forceful and impatient or timid and tolerant is partially determined by the type of body we have.

Each of our bodies comes complete with skills and talents that we can use to good purpose, as well as faults and weaknesses which are a challenge for us to overcome. As will be described in Chapter 3, the body's temperamental tendencies can be strongly influenced by the other parts of our personalities.

THE FACT OF OUR physical existence itself depends on the continued functioning of our bodies. Some people believe that when the body dies, the rest of personality also ceases to exist. Others have come to different conclusions.

One thing is certain; when the body's tissues wear out and it can no longer carry on its usual functions, our physical existence stops short. What happens to the other parts of personality at that point is a fascinating question, one which we shall take up in later chapters.

IT IS IMPORTANT to understand that the different parts of personality, in more or less direct ways, all have their origin in God. For example, science indicates that the human body is actually the result of millions of years of slow, steady evolution. But evolution itself is not a random accident. It is a planned and purposeful process guided by a higher spiritual Presence. Our minds are, in a similar fashion, and more directly, given to us by God.

THE MYSTERIOUS MIND

Much confusion has characterized our attempts to understand the difference between the mind and the physical brain. Some thinkers argue that the brain is all there is and that thought is nothing more than electro-chemical activity within it. Others claim that there has to be something additional to the brain, some essence that actually coordinates thoughts. If we have separate and nonphysical minds, how do they work together with our physical brains?

It seems likely that our minds are separate thought-processing systems, and they are intricately linked to our physical brains. In a sense, the nonphysical mind rests upon and hooks up with the physical foundation of the brain. To illustrate this arrangement let's take an ordinary series of thoughts and trace its path.

A man is walking through the woods. He enters a clearing where he suddenly sees an old friend whom he has not met in several years. His eyes carry this visual stimulus along nerve channels to his brain where an incredibly complex series of electro-chemical activities occur. At the same time that all this neural activity is occurring in his physical brain, much is happening on the associated level of his mind.

Corresponding to the many electrical impulses going on in his brain, his mind is experiencing actual thoughts, memories, and feelings about his old friend. The mind is the part of him that experiences on the usual level of everyday awareness.

When he sees his friend he does not experience a sentimental electrical impulse or a memorable chemical transformation; he experiences actual thoughts and memories, and he experiences them directly in his mind.

These thought reactions are quite real for him. They are what his mind handles day in and day out, his everyday reality. While it is true that his mind is connected to the electrical activity of his physical brain, it is the mind level of which he is normally aware. His brain registers thoughts electrically on the physical level; his mind experiences thoughts directly on the level of conscious awareness.

HOW THE MIND WORKS

Mind serves as the center of our conscious awareness. It is the main stage upon which the daily events of our inner lives unfold. It is where we experience the reality of day-to-day living. The part of us that is aware of ourselves and the world around us is the mind. Our sense of self, of identity, is rooted within our minds.

MIND INHERENTLY TIES OUR thoughts and experiences together. It works like a spider, busily connecting thoughts to each other with webs of meaning. When a new experience or thought comes to us, the first thing that mind tries to do is unify that thought, tie it in with the rest of what it already contains. It takes the thought, connects it with other thoughts, and discovers new meaningful relationships between them.

But what guides this amazing process of unification? Our minds certainly do more than simply connect thoughts to other thoughts in a totally random fashion. They are guided and purposeful as they unify incoming reality.

That essence which is responsible for the direction of the mind's work is human will. Will, the power to choose, decide, and act, is centered in our minds. In fact, will *is* the directing essence within mind.

MIND IS THE CENTRAL switchboard of personality. Our awareness, our sense of self, and our will all center in the mind. It is natural that the functions of the other parts of personality should be coordinated there as well. Body, soul, and Spirit all hook into this central switchboard of the mind. There the will can direct them in the balanced functioning of the unified personality.

IN SUMMARY THEN, our minds have three functions which are basic to their very nature. First, mind is the place where our conscious awareness exists. Second, mind unifies new thoughts with the rest of what it contains. It does so in a directed and purposeful manner because of will which exists within it. And third, mind is the coordinating switchboard for the rest of personality.

MAN IS MORE than simply a body and mind. These are but the foundation for the higher parts of personality, Spirit and soul. Chapter 2 explores the nature of Spirit and soul, the role that they play in our everyday lives, and their importance to how our personalities continue on in the afterlife.

CHAPTER

2

The Inner Spirit and the Evolving Soul

THE WORKINGS OF BODY AND MIND ALONE explain some of the life of an average human being. But then so much of what we are and do would remain a complete mystery if that was as deep as we looked.

Why does a hungry man share his small portion of food with a friend? How can a person know that one thing is right and another is wrong? Why is it that people in every culture, from the most primitive to the most sophisticated, have sought and worshipped something higher and unseen? To answer such questions we must look beyond body and mind to the highest parts of human nature.

God has not left us alone in our struggle to reach for higher things. To each of us He has sent a fragment of Himself, to love us and to work for our spiritual enlightenment. Residing within each of our personalities, these inner Spirit-fragments, these sparks of infinity, are devoted to working patiently, ceaselessly, to show us the true spiritual values that are woven throughout the fabric of our daily lives.

In response to the ministry of these God-fragments within us, something utterly amazing begins to happen. In the higher reaches of human nature a new part of personality is born: the spiritual self, the soul. As the inner Spirit-guide compiles the spiritual insights of living, this soul matures and evolves. As a sculptor applies bits of clay and slowly shapes his work, so the inner Spirit artfully combines the experiences of life and forms them into a living soul. In this chapter we will journey to the heights of human nature in an exploration of the inner Spirit and the evolving soul.

THE INNER SPIRIT: A FRAGMENT OF GOD

There is an important point that should be clarified right at the outset of this discussion on the inner Spirit. For convenience, the Spirit has been loosely referred to as part of human personality. The Spirit-fragment is not actually a part of man, but rather a part of God. In fact, for all intents and purposes, the inner Spirit *is* God to each human being.

So, to be more accurate, the Spirit-fragment is a presence that works within human personality, rather than an actual part of that personality. In contrast, the body, mind, and soul are actual parts of the person. This is a most important distinction. While it is correct to say that a part of God dwells within man, it is utterly wrong to say that man is God.

THE MOST STRIKING, the most awesome evidence of the Father's love for His children is that He has given a part of Himself to each one of us. This inner Spirit which works in the depths of our minds is an actual fragment of the Creator of the entire universe, and is perfect in every way.

Thus God is much more to us than merely some vast and far-away force. His individual Spirit presence is the deepest and most intimate reality within each human personality. Because He is right inside of us, He is closer and more accessible to us than any other person or thing that exists.

The task of this God-fragment is to spiritualize the human personality. The Spirit is the inner compass which ever points toward higher truth, the dedicated Teacher, the perfect Guide that leads each of us along the eternal path to the Creator.

These inner Spirits are working constantly at every moment of our lives to show us God's Will. Each time we move through an experience, they strive to convey to our human minds the spiritual truths to be gained from that experience. They never cease their efforts. They are totally and perfectly dedicated to the spiritual advancement of the human beings which they indwell.

These God-fragments are devoted to our growth and welfare with a love that is overwhelming, the very love that the Father has for each of His spiritual children. And if we offer them our cooperation, they will lead us forward through this life and beyond, along an eternal adventure of coming increasingly to know and love the infinite God which is at once our source and our ultimate destiny.

The presence of the Spirit within us is God's guarantee, the assurance of His commitment to us. If we sincerely desire to find the Father and if we persist in our efforts, there is nothing in the entire universe that can stop us from succeeding. For a part of the God of all creation lives within each of us, leading us toward an ever greater understanding of His infinite nature. Within each of us a revelation is unfolding, if only we will open up our hearts and minds to receive it.

HOW THE INNER SPIRIT WORKS

There is an old saying that goes, "You can lead a horse to water, but you can't make him drink." That may be true, but you can surely make him thirsty. And that is part of what the inner Spirit-fragments try to do within human personality. They try to stimulate our thirst for spiritual truth.

They encourage us to wonder about ourselves and the universe around us, to reach for the deeper meanings and values that lie beneath the surface of commonplace living. They constantly fan the flame of our search for the perfect Source of all that is true, beautiful, and good.

But at the same time that these Spirit-guides encourage our thirst for truth, they also pour forth the very spiritual waters for which our souls are yearning. They refresh us with higher wisdom.

When we encounter a difficult life situation and we sincerely desire to understand the right way to proceed, the inner Spirit-guides represent to us what God would have us do. If we persistently seek their leading, they can show us the Father's Will for each unique moment in our lives. They attempt to communicate the spiritual insights which we need in each particular situation.

THE WORK OF THE SPIRIT in personality should not be confused with the workings of conscience. Conscience is a function of the human mind. It is merely the storehouse of past experiences of right and wrong absorbed from our culture and family life. While much of worth is stored in the conscience, it is still only a limited set of human values and ideals. Conscience is simply a reminder of old lessons learned.

The inner Spirit on the other hand is the *very essence* of living truth. The Spirit's mission is to reveal new and illuminating truth, to lead us forward into previously uncharted regions of spiritual discovery, to lure us on to ever greater achievements on the thrilling frontiers of spiritual living. While conscience preserves our past progress, the inner Spirit leads us into the growth of the future.

NORMALLY WE ARE not much aware of the work of the Spirit within our personalities. The plants in a garden are not "aware" of the gardener or how he does his work. Yet they are much benefited by his efforts. Similarly, we are rarely conscious of the actual presence of the inner Spirit-guides or of how they do their work. They function at a level that is higher than the everyday awareness of our minds. They work at super-conscious levels, above our normal awareness, trying to influence our conscious thinking toward spiritual conclusions. What we usually are aware of is the *results* of their efforts, rather than of the efforts themselves.

Perhaps an illustration from everyday life can further clarify this point. Suppose a harried counter clerk at a department store makes an impatient and nasty reply to a question you have asked him. Your immediate impulse is to reply with a nasty remark of your own. But you check this urge and ask for spiritual insight and self-control to deal with this difficult situation.

Your mind begins to calm and steady. You pause for a few moments and then find yourself able to reply with caring and patience to soothe the hard-pressed clerk and redirect the situation along more loving lines.

Let's look more closely at what happened during those few moments. The inner Spirit, as always, was working outside of your conscious awareness in the super-conscious levels of your personality, trying to show you the higher way to handle the situation. By requesting spiritual guidance you were able consciously to receive the insights and strength you needed to act in a higher way. You were probably not directly aware of the inner Guide's activities in those important moments, but you certainly were aware of the valuable results of the Spirit's work in your mind.

As often as we request God's guidance with persistence and a sincere heart, we can expect to receive uplifting inspiration from His inner Spirit.

THE INTENSITY OF the mightiest hurricane pales in comparison to the intensity of God's love for man. It is the inner God-fragments that carry the fullness of the Father's love directly to each one of us. The Spirit within serves us with infinite compassion and wisdom. If we wish, we can begin to experience the mighty transformations that result from living in intimate association with God's inner Presence.

BEYOND THEIR WORK of elevating the lives of individuals, these indwelling Spirit-fragments have had a tremendous influence on the forward movement of human civilization as a whole. Their collective influence is largely responsible for man's development from little more than an animal to his present plateau of material and spiritual achievement. They have nurtured all that is true, beautiful, and good in evolving human society. And they will continue to provide the inspiration which will move civilization forward over the long road ahead, toward the golden ages of spiritual flowering that our world is destined to reach in the centuries to come.

ONE OF THE MOST important activities of the inner Spirit concerns the survival of our personalities after death. The Spirit is unaffected by the death of the body. The inner Guide functions in the higher nonphysical areas of personality.

Throughout our lives, the Spirit-fragments work continuously to stimulate and preserve everything of spiritual value in our human experience. With this accumulating wealth the Spirit labors to construct a higher spiritual self, an enduring soul that is capable of surviving physical death.

When the earth-bound caterpillar has reached a certain point in its development, it spins a cocoon and drifts into a death-like sleep. Time passes. The cocoon breaks open. A brilliant lace-winged butterfly emerges and floats delicately off with the wind currents, leaving the shell of its birth behind.

Similarly, when our human bodies break down, our personalities move into a new stage of existence. The center of our self-awareness shifts from the dying mind to the evolving soul. The physical shell is left behind. And the spiritually delicate soul, with its associated Spirit-guide, lifts off into the afterlife as the transformed personality of one-time earthly existence.

SOUL: THE EVOLVING HIGHER SELF

The soul is a most amazing part of human personality. It is our nonphysical, spiritual self which is destined to survive physical death and become the center of personality in the after-life.

The soul grows as the result of the combined efforts of the human mind and the inner Spirit. The mind provides a constant supply of the raw materials of living experience. Working within the mind, the Spirit winnows out every bit of this living experience that is of any spiritual worth. Out of this mass of living spiritual experience, the Spirit initiates and nurtures the soul. Throughout our lives, whenever an experience of spiritual import occurs, the Spirit faithfully integrates it into the evolving soul.

As our lives unfold, if we choose to live spiritually, our souls will have an increasing number of experiences stored within them. As they thus gather spiritual substance, our souls evolve the survival stature that makes them ready to become the center of our personalities after physical death. This earthly life is a sort of pregnancy period during which the embryonic soul develops to the point where, at physical death, it is "delivered" into the spiritual existence in which it was meant to live.

Have you ever watched airplanes taxiing on a runway at the airport? They are not there just to taxi around indefinitely. They travel down the runway in order to gather speed for take-off into the open skies, their true element. So it is with our souls. This physical life is the experiential runway over which our souls travel to pick up the spiritual momentum they need to lift off into their new existence in the after-life.

IT IS IMPORTANT to keep clear the distinction between the soul and the Spirit. The Spirit, a fragment of God *residing within* human personality, is perfect and divine in origin. The Spirit's purpose is to guide the personality Godward. In contrast, the soul is a *part of* human personality; it is the finite and growing higher self.

JUST AS IT IS the natural function of our minds to deal with intellectual facts and meanings, so our souls work naturally with spiritual values and ideals. The soul is that part of personality which inherently responds to spiritual truth. Much as our eyes sense a color and our minds understand a meaning, our souls directly feel spiritual values such as generosity or courage. In fact, it is with our souls that we perceive God, that we directly sense the presence of His inner Spirit.

IT IS MOST IMPORTANT to recognize that the soul is a dynamic, growing element in personality. To some extent it is like a living muscle in the human body which, if it is not exercised properly, begins to wither away. Our souls are not static like blocks of stone. They are either growing or shrinking. Either they are healthy and vibrant or they are poorly developed and weak.

The state of the soul determines whether the personality itself has enough reality to continue on after physical death. If, like a premature infant, the soul is weak and "underweight", its chances for survival in the afterlife are slim.

THE STRENGTH OF THE SOUL depends most directly on the decisions and actions taken by will during the course of human life. If we choose, we can willfully seek the leading of the inner Spirit. We can direct our personalities along paths of robust spiritual living, and thus add nourishing substance to our souls. We can keep our souls vibrant and growing.

On the other hand, we can wilfully choose to avoid the challenges and responsibilities of the higher life. We can retreat into the cave of a shallow and meaningless existence. In such circumstances our souls and, in fact, our entire personalities wither under the direction of a weak and misguided will.

In the next chapter we will explore the nature of the will and the part that it plays in the development of a strong, balanced, and unified personality.

CHAPTER

3

Human Will and the Unified Personality

IN THE PSYCHOLOGICALLY HEALTHY human being all the parts of personality work together in a unified fashion. For exploration purposes we have considered body, mind, Spirit, and soul separately, but as we normally go through life we are not aware of these parts as separate. Usually we are more aware of ourselves functioning as whole personalities.

There come times, however, when we are not working quite so smoothly, when we do not feel quite so whole. Conflicts arise within our personalities. Higher spiritual values battle with lower emotions and urges.

Such struggles come to each of us; they are inherent in the process of living. Resolving such internal conflicts is the role of will. Will holds the reins of personality control; will has the power to unify body, mind, and soul under the perfect guidance of the inner Spirit.

WILL AT THE CONTROLS

Future students of human nature will look back at our times and wonder how we could have been so blind. We have been guilty of largely overlooking one of the most crucial elements in human personality. Will lies at the very center of personality. If mind is the central switchboard, then it is will that sits at the controls.

It is will which most clearly distinguishes a human being from the animal level of existence. An animal registers and coordinates perceptions. A human being has an additional ability. He can consciously reflect on his perceptions in a self-directed manner. If an animal that is thirsty sees a pool of water, it drinks. A thirsty human being would also drink. But then he would probably reflect a bit on his situation and proceed to find a way to store some water for the time when he would again be thirsty.

Using his will, man reaches conscious conclusions and makes purposeful decisions which guide his actions. This process occurs in a fully developed form only in man. Will is thoroughly woven into the fabric of human mind. Wherever the normal human level of mind exists, will functions within it.

Will is the vital spark which mobilizes us. It is the force which moves us through reality. Using will, we choose, decide, and initiate action. Any move that we make starts with the will. When I stretch out my hand to pick up a pencil, it is with my will that I decide to do it. When I develop an intellectual theory or express love for a friend, I engage in an act of will.

It is will which makes each of us a creative force within reality. Will empowers us to have an impact on, to change, the reality in which we live. The better developed our wills, the greater is our impact on people and events around us. The less developed our wills, the more we will be influenced and controlled by people and events around us.

The same principle holds true for the inner life. The stronger our wills, the more unified and directed are the emotions and thoughts of our inner lives. The weaker our wills, the greater is the tendency toward confusion and conflict between the multiple urges and thoughts within our personalities.

THE EFFECT OF EXTREME will deterioration on personality can be seen in those unfortunate people who have spent years on the back wards of our mental hospitals. Over a period of time, will abdicates its role as director of the mental and emotional life. Emotions and thoughts collide in increasing chaos under tremendous pressures. Eventually, the personality is left shattered. What remains is a drifting, splintered shell, a tragic remnant of what was once a whole person.

It should be realized, however, that at any point short of total will deterioration a person can turn things around, can rally his will, can take command of his life once more and begin progressing toward vigorous and unified personality functioning. At first, his mental and emotional problems will persist because his will is unskilled at directing his personality. It's as if he is rolling downhill on a bicycle and decides he wants to head back up to the top. He first has to brake to a stop, and then he can turn around and start pedaling uphill.

Having slid for a ways downhill, it is difficult to turn around and head in the right direction. But if a person persists, his ability to guide himself toward more unified ways of living will improve markedly. Will reacts to use; if we use it often, it becomes strong and skillful; if we use it seldom, it becomes weak and ineffective.

WHEN WE ACT willfully, we usually do so in a two-stage process. First we act within the inner life. When we struggle with a difficult choice and come to a clear decision, we are exercising our wills within the inner environment of our minds. Having formulated this inner resolve, we must then move to the second stage of will function, and translate our inner decisions to actions in the outer life of events and relationships.

Take, for example, the shy young man struggling with the decision to ask the girl he likes out for a date. First he reaches an inner resolve to ask her. Then he acts in the outer life by actually calling her and asking the big question.

In order for the will to develop and maintain its proper role as the director of personality, we must act strongly in both the inner life of thoughts, emotions, and decisions, and in the outer life of actions. Our inner change and growth is meaningful only if the outer lives we live reflect this inner development. If will function is to be healthy, we must apply it in a balanced fashion in both our inner and outer lives.

THE EFFECTIVE WILL ACTS

The function of will is to deliberate, decide and act. When over a period of time we fail to carry out these functions, our wills become weak and semi-paralyzed. It is well to remember the story of the hungry donkey sitting between two bales of hay. Each bale was an equal distance from him, and he could not decide which one to approach. He kept looking from one to the other, unable to decide, and eventually died of starvation.

We must exercise our wills. To not choose and not act is destructive to the health of personality. Sometimes, when dealing with a difficult decision, we may have a hard time finding a satisfactory solution. But if we have covered the issues carefully, it is important not to delay the making and carrying out of a decision indefinitely.

You cannot steer a car unless it is moving. If it is moving in the wrong direction you can slow it down, turn it around, and move it in the right direction. But first you have to get it moving.

The dynamic personality guided by an active will can always correct itself as it grows. But it cannot correct itself and grow if it is unmoving. The healthy personality has a dynamic and effective will at its core. And the effective will acts.

FREE WILL MEANS RESPONSIBILITY

The fact that will has control in personality means that a human being has primary responsibility for the direction of his life. Of course, it is true that environment has an impact on us; important people and events do influence us to a substantial degree. But the most powerful factor in determining how happy and fulfilled we can be is the nature of the decisions and actions we choose.

There is no negative influence in life that is so powerful that it cannot be overcome by persistent decisions and actions designed to remedy it. Given time, will inevitably triumphs over circumstance.

As a matter of fact, there is no such thing as free will without responsibility. When we choose and decide recklessly, with abandon, without awareness and responsibility, we are in the most real sense shackled by circumstance.

For instance, the transient person who lives on the streets takes no responsibility for himself or his actions. Some might argue that because he has no obligations he is entirely free. But in actuality his life is severely limited. He is imprisoned by his own lack of self-control. It is when we responsibly control and guide our lives that we experience the greatest freedom.

GOD'S WILL AND MAN'S WILL

It is God who is the author of all reality. Being the infinite and original personality, the Father has willed the existence of all things and beings. Just as we control the direction of our individual lives by our human will decisions, so the Father controls the ultimate destiny of the universe by His divine and all-powerful Will.

Along with the gift of personality which the Father has so generously provided for each of us, He has also given us the priceless gift of personal free will. Volition, the right to control and guide reality, has its origin in God. To each one of us the Father has entrusted a piece of His Will prerogative, a human-sized chunk of free will. The very existence we lead is ours to control. We have the right to guide our own growth. We each have the privilege of determining our own destiny.

BUT WHY HAS the Father given us such power? Having the right of self-determination, what shall we do with ourselves? The key lies in recognizing that God has a superb purpose for our lives. At any one time, in any particular circumstance, the Father knows the perfect and right way for us to be.

God has a Will for our lives, both at the level of everyday particulars and at the level of overall life direction. Whether we are simply sharing with a friend or making an important life decision, we have the option of searching for the Father's Will in that situation and trying to live it out.

We can seek higher leading, the leading of the Father's inner guiding Spirit. The Spirit-fragments work constantly to represent the Father's Will to our minds as we move through the process of daily life. These perfect Guides *are* the Will of God within us.

This is where our human wills exercise their greatest power. We can choose either to accept or reject God's Will for us. God knows what is the best, the highest course for our lives, and He desires that we follow His Will. However, He never forces us to choose His Will. By giving us free will, He has given us full control over our choices. We can either seek earnestly to understand and do His Will, or we can ignore His spiritual leading and exclusively follow our own limited human wills (which reminds me irrepressibly of a dog chasing its own tail).

The highest possible function of human will occurs when we choose to align it with the perfect Will of the Father. The choicest gift we can give to God is our loving desire to become more like Him, to live according to the guidance of His inner Spirit.

When we choose to do God's Will, we choose God Himself. We reach for the highest values of truth, beauty, and goodness. We begin an endless adventure of exploration into reality.

If we choose to ignore the Father's leading, we choose in the long run to abandon reality, for God is reality. When man rejects God he chooses to become increasingly self-centered and self-circumscribed, and thus increasingly unreal. Eventually the God-rejecting individual loses all reality and ceases to exist.

C. S. Lewis, in his book *The Great Divorce*, describes God as holding man like a glowing coal in the palm of His hand, breathing on it to make it flame. But if the coal will not flame, it eventually dies out leaving nothing but ashes. And when God blows, the ashes scatter to the winds. Such is the fate of the human will which isolates itself from its source.

SOME MIGHT COMPLAIN that to do God's Will they have to give up some of their own will; they lose control over their lives.

But doing God's Will is not at all a matter of sacrificing our own wills. Instead we freely and wholeheartedly decide to dedicate our human wills to the doing of the Will of the Father. It is an enlarging rather than a narrowing of our freedom, an expansion of human will by alliance with the divine Will. It's as if we plug ourselves into an outlet that has an infinite power supply of wisdom and strength.

As human will begins to align with God's Will, the choices available to that human will become more broad and full. The options for real, worthwhile activity increase. The scope of our freedom grows.

Insofar as we reject God's Will, life's possibilities become more narrow. Our increasingly isolated human wills have less and less to choose from that is of any lasting value. Our options become petty and limited in scope. The circle of our freedom shrinks. True freedom means eternal enlargement, never-ending growth toward God. God is infinitely larger, greater, more real than a human being. When we refuse to follow God, it is as if we shut ourselves into a small room. We surround ourselves by our own tiny boundaries and ultimately cut ourselves off from real and lasting freedom.

KNOWING GOD'S WILL

God, through His inner Spirit presence, is constantly attempting to show us His Will. The extent to which these attempts penetrate our everyday awareness depends on human will.

Our minds are naturally attuned to everyday material functions: getting up in the morning, getting ready for work, feeding the kids, paying the bills. The Spirit's task of showing us the Father's Will is indeed difficult when our minds are thus constantly filled with everyday activities and concerns.

But we have the power to direct the functioning of our minds. We can choose to order the priorities of our mental activity and set time aside for communion with the inner Spirit. We can make room in our minds for the Spirit's input, even in the midst of everyday activities. It's much like tuning in the station we want on the radio. We move our thoughts off of everyday matters for a time, and tune our minds to the inner "wavelength" of the Spirit.

IN THE BEGINNING it is often difficult for us to sense the subtle leadings of the inner Spirit. When we first attempt contact with God, our minds are poorly trained to receive such guidance. Once again the importance of human will becomes apparent. We must willfully direct our minds to spiritual pursuits.

The only way that an apprentice carpenter becomes a full-fledged professional is to work persistently at his trade for a number of years. Similarly, the only way that we improve our ability to sense God's presence and understand His Will is to persevere, to keep on trying to reach God.

Over a period of time, as we continue to experiment in the inner life, continue to try one way and then another of building a relationship with the Father, our minds develop heightened sensitivity to the presence of God's inner Spirit. We grow attuned to the flow of spiritual insight coming from that Presence.

The stronger our desire to know God and the longer we persist in God-reaching efforts, the more skilled our minds become at sensing and cooperating with the inner Spirit. The more we attempt to know God's Will, the better we become at discerning it. Spiritual insight does not happen automatically; it must be consciously pursued and developed.

DOING GOD'S WILL

It is not enough to simply *know* God's Will. That is only the first step. We must also *do* God's Will. There is an important difference between hearing a song and singing it. After understanding truth, the necessary next step is to actually live out that truth, to carry it into action.

It is our privilege not only to understand the truth intellectually with our minds, but to become the truth experientially with our entire personalities. Each time our human wills implement the divine Will, we become God-like in one more small way. Each experience of living out the Father's Will brings us one tiny step closer to perfection.

THE PSYCHOLOGICAL IMPACT OF DOING GOD'S WILL

When we whole-heartedly dedicate ourselves to knowing and doing God's Will, tremendous changes begin to transpire in our personalities. Such transformations rarely happen suddenly; they are not always evident in any single day or in any single act. But as days pass to months and years, the results of such attempts to live out the Father's Will emerge as clearly noticeable. Time helps them stand out as an obvious and increasing pattern of God-like living.

When we become thus spiritually remotivated, our very deepest desire is to seek and carry out the Will of the Father. All other motivations take second place to this supreme desire to live the way God wishes us to live. We thus make choices and determine personality actions in accordance with the guidance of the inner Spirit.

When we make such a primary consecration of our human wills, we start on the road to unifying and harmonizing our personalities. We leave conflicting motives and behaviors behind as we coordinate our personalities around the axis of the Father's Will. The planets of our solar system don't collide with each other. They are lined up in an orderly way by the gravity pull of the sun. Similarly, as we pursue God's Will, the various urges and drives of our personalities are lined up by the inner gravity pull of the Father's Spirit.

As we reach for God's Will, we begin to develop a working partnership with His inner Presence. We begin to experience the rewards of reaching for higher purposes. Increasingly we are transformed by the indescribable joy of living as children of the eternal God.

THE BALANCED PERSONALITY

A major key to psychological health lies in maintaining a balanced function among the various parts of personality. When our wills are strong and wise, we can properly coordinate the functions of the body, mind, soul, and Spirit in a harmonious interplay. To the extent that the influence of any of the parts is overemphasized, the balance of personality suffers.

The indulgence of our physical natures can overly dominate to the point of deteriorating our mental and spiritual lives. We can become so involved with eating, sex, bodily comfort, and other physical concerns, that we ignore intellectual pursuits such as reading, writing, and theorizing, and spiritual activities such as worship, meditation, and loving relationships.

Similarly, we can become so immersed in intellectual pursuits that our bodies are ill-cared for and our spiritual lives neglected. Spiritual overdevelopment can be equally disastrous. It breeds an unbalanced fanaticism that has resulted in everything from people starving themselves trying to attain "mystical" states, to "holy" wars of conversion which have destroyed entire cultures.

The physical, mental, and spiritual elements in personality act as vital checks and balances on each other. Body and mind keep the spiritual life rooted in daily reality. They act as a braking and stabilizing force on extreme spiritual urges. At the same time Spirit and soul provide the depth and purpose we need to guide our everyday living.

DO YOU REMEMBER what it is like to look at the surface of a deep still pool of water? At first you see simply the reflection on its surface. But then your perspective shifts and suddenly you see beyond the surface into the depths of the pond: dark green tendrils of moss, darting fish, shadowed nooks and hollows, an entirely different world.

Similarly, with the body senses and the mind we perceive only the material and intellectual surface of reality. When we explore with the spiritual vision of the soul, aided by the indwelling Spirit, we see beyond the mere surface of reality into its depths. When the parts of our personalities function together in balance, then we can live on multiple levels of reality simultaneously.

THE BALANCED FUNCTIONING of the body plays an important role in the overall balance of the personality. Bodily states can strongly affect how receptive we are to the leadings of the Spirit. If we are physically exhausted, have not slept or eaten properly, or have been seriously ill, our minds will probably be unclear and our emotions unstable and overly sensitive. Such abnormal states can distort or block our receptivity to the subtle inspirations of the Spirit.

Spirit influence on personality is enhanced by the mental and emotional stability which results from balanced body energies. Regular and healthful patterns of rest, nutrition, and physical activity lead to that balanced functioning of our bodies which is most conducive to our total growth.

IN FURTHER CONSIDERING personality balance, it is important to realize that the inner Spirit does not attempt to have an extreme impact on our minds. Shattering spiritual trumpet blasts would only serve to disorient and inflame our personalities. Extreme spiritual urges can send us into tailspins of religious fanaticism.

Instead, the leading of the Spirit-fragment is usually muted and subtle so as to allow us to assimilate the communicated spiritual truth in a balanced way. The Spirit's input to our minds usually emerges over a period of time through efforts that are patient and persistent. The Spirit's ministry is purposefully measured so as not to disrupt the equilibrium of our thinking.

If spiritual insight is balanced, it corresponds with our highest intellectual and emotional understandings. It matches up with the lessons we have learned in earlier life experiences. And true spiritual leading fits in well with the non-spiritual areas of our lives. It does not overwhelm the rest of personality. It enhances our overall stable progress.

ANOTHER FACTOR that contributes to personality balance is spiritual momentum. As we continue to make spiritual choices and decisions over a period of time and our souls accumulate this growing store of spiritual experience, we begin to build spiritual momentum. Having made spiritual decisions in the past, it becomes easier for us to make even more powerful spiritual decisions in the present and future. Such spiritual momentum results in a stronger and more balanced personality.

Consider the spinning top. If it continues to spin, to maintain its momentum, it remains balanced and upright. If it loses its momentum, it begins to wobble and fall. Similarly, by maintaining our spiritual momentum, we remain balanced and upright. If we become spiritually lazy and inconsistent, we lose our spiritual momentum and eventually begin to wobble and fall.

LIFE'S THREE LEVELS: FACT, MEANING, AND VALUE

We experience life on three different levels: *fact, meaning,* and *value.*

Our bodies register physical *facts.* We see a sunset, hear the chirping of birds, feel the rough bark of a tree.

Our minds connect these separate facts with webs of *meaning.* The sun keeps the birds warm and helps the tree to grow.

The Spirit reveals the deeper *values* of reality. The underlying beauty of the plan which links sun, birds, trees, and man together is a value which we feel with our souls.

Facts would have no import without the meaning-connections we discover with our minds. Likewise, meanings take on an additional depth when we associate them with Spirit-inspired values. The inner Spirit uses facts and meanings as raw material in generating spiritual values. Such values exist in a dimension beyond the levels of fact and meaning.

Human personality can experience life on all three of these levels. We can interweave facts, meanings, and values into a rich tapestry of dynamic living.

To further illustrate such a full-spectrum functioning of personality, let us look in on the scene of a father and his young child at a playground. The child has just fallen and scraped his knee and is wailing loudly as his Dad picks him up and tries to comfort him.

Our bodily senses perceive several facts. The child is crying; the man is holding him; the man is speaking to the child; the child's crying begins to subside; the man hugs the child and continues to speak to him; the child's cries slowly reduce to a whimper; the man puts the child down; the child begins playing on the swings; the man smiles.

Our bodies send all these sensory facts to our minds which immediately tie them together with meanings. The man is the child's father; the child is frightened and hurt; the father is attempting to comfort the child; the child is dependent on his father for help, and wants to be comforted; the father is effective at soothing the child. Our minds draw all these meanings from the perceived facts.

At this point, the inner Spirit can dimensionally deepen these meanings with spiritual value insights. The father and child love each other; the father is sympathetic to the child's hurt; he knows it will pass but feels compassion for the child's present distress; the father's devotion is good and beautiful; the child trusts the goodness and love of his father; our divine Father relates to us in similar though perfect ways when we, His mortal children, are hurt in the process of living; just as this human father tries to comfort his child our spiritual Father tries to comfort us and show us the transiency of our pain. All these are value insights that the Spirit can superimpose upon the facts and meanings inherent in the scene we are witnessing.

The richness of fact, meaning, and value that we experience depends on the human will. We can walk by our father-child tableau with our only reaction being one of annoyance at the cries of the child. Alternatively, we can pause for thirty seconds and experience the whole broad range of facts, meanings, and values previously described, and probably more, if we choose to.

By our will decisions, we determine how much precious meaning and value we refine from the raw ore of living experience. We can set our minds to generating meanings and can invite the value inspiration of the inner Spirit. If we choose, we can be highly active on all three levels of fact, meaning, and value.

THE EMOTIONS

Even a brief review of the current psychological literature points out an unfortunate trend: while the role of will in personality has been underemphasized, the role of the emotions has been highlighted out of all proportion to its real importance in the psychological life. We are not at the mercy of our emotional flows. Personality does not merely tag along behind a barely tamed vortex of raw feelings. In fact, in the mature personality the situation is reversed. Will and Spirit set the course and the emotions are channeled in line with higher purposes.

EMOTIONS ARE FEELING reactions to reality that have an impact on all the parts of personality. When we experience positive emotions such as love or joy our bodies are invigorated, our minds clarified, and our souls expanded. The Spirit can reveal deeper insights to us when our hearts are opened by such higher emotions.

Negative emotions such as anger or fear have an equally profound but opposite effect on personality. They deteriorate our bodies, poison our minds, shrivel our souls, and block Spirit input.

While emotions affect all parts of personality, each time an emotion occurs it *originates* in a particular part of personality. There are thus three separate types of emotion; those that start in the body, those that start in the mind, and those that have their origin in the higher parts of personality, the soul and Spirit.

Examples of body-origin emotions are sexual arousal, or the fear we would feel on encountering a large rattlesnake in the woods. Such emotions start as an instinctive physiological reaction in our bodies.

Emotions originating in our minds start with a thought process; for example, appreciation for the work of a colleague, or anger at having one's car stolen.

Examples of spiritual emotions are the outpouring of joy we can feel in worship, or the mustering of courage in the face of difficulty, or loving someone who has been less than pleasant to us. These emotions originate in Spirit inspiration.

WILL AND THE EMOTIONS

We can willfully determine the tenor of our emotional lives. When our emotions are drifting in a destructive direction, we can look for higher emotional insight. We have the option of shifting the source of our emotional perspective from the body or mind to the inner Spirit.

Emotional poisons such as anger, fear, envy, hatred and pride place communication blocks between the Spirit and the rest of personality. We can either sit idly by while such emotions cause havoc within us or we can work to dissipate such negative emotions. We can willfully open the way for the Spirit to inspire higher emotions to replace them.

THERE IS A NATURAL momentum to our emotional lives. Picture a boat on a fast-flowing river. The river has powerful currents. If someone controls the rudder of the boat firmly, the boat can use the river's momentum to move forward rapidly. If, however, there is no one at the rudder the boat will be tossed and smashed by the force of the river.

If we are weak-willed, we allow our personalities to be tossed about and damaged by emotional cross-currents. If we use our wills in a strong and intelligent manner, we can harness our natural emotional momentum to further the progress of the whole personality.

WE CAN PURSUE emotional self-control in three stages. In the first stage it is crucial that we recognize and acknowledge negative emotions if we are presently experiencing them. It is destructive simply to suppress such emotions. The first step in changing anger or fear is to admit to ourselves that we are angry or afraid, and to understand as fully as possible why we feel that way.

Having done this we can safely move to the second stage. We evaluate our feelings and decide whether it is right for us to continue feeling anger or fear. If we decide to leave them behind we move on to the third stage, where we work to cultivate higher, more worthwhile emotions.

In this third stage of cultivating higher emotions, there is a point that is crucial to keep in mind: the idea is not to suppress or push away the negative emotions. Instead we should concentrate on developing alternative positive emotions by seeking the guidance of the inner Spirit. As the positive emotions grow, the negative emotions will slip increasingly into the background and eventually become inactive. We cannot eject undesirable emotions by sheer force of will. But they will naturally abate when we develop positive emotions to replace them.

ONE OF THE MOST powerful forces for emotional self-transformation is prayer. We can pray sincerely for insight and courage to do God's Will in an emotionally trying situation. By praying we widen the channel of love, strength, and wisdom which can flow to us from the Father's inner Spirit. When we initiate such sincere prayer, mighty emotional transformations can occur.

ONE OF THE MOST damaging psychological misconceptions that is prevalent in our modern view of human nature is that our inner emotions are determined largely by the outer circumstances which happen to surround us. If we hear sad news we automatically become depressed. If someone is pestering us we inevitably become angry. Our psychology gurus tell us to express our feelings, to "go with the flow" of these emotional reactions to circumstance.

Unfortunately, such advice ignores the critical responsibility of will in the emotional life. We can willfully guide our emotions in a more uplifting, a more real direction even in the midst of an adverse situation. The state of our inner environment need not depend directly on the circumstances of our outer environment.

Of course, if something sad happens we will feel somewhat sad at first. We cannot and should not ignore such emotions. However, having acknowledged such "natural" feelings, it is the proper function of will to seek a higher spiritual outlook on the situation. We can transform our inner emotions in response to such a higher perspective.

We are not limited to reacting passively to an outer situation. We can actively choose what is desirable emotionally, and reach for such a higher outlook. We can actively determine our inner emotional environment according to the leading of the Spirit.

THE READER MAY HAVE noted the above reference to sad feelings in a sad situation as being "natural". This term deserves some explanation.

Emotions that originate in the everyday parts of our personalities, the mind and body, arise more or less automatically in reaction to outer events. Such emotions occur "naturally". Anger at stubbing your toe, elation at winning a thousand dollars in a contest; these are natural and automatic emotional reactions. Will plays little part in such emotions. They do not originate as a result of our conscious choices; they happen spontaneously.

In contrast to such "naturally" occurring emotions, we consciously choose the higher emotional insights that originate in the Spirit and soul. We recognize the desirability of such emotions as hope, love, courage, and joy, and we willfully cultivate them.

If will is inactive in the emotional life, we do little reaching for higher emotions. The "natural" emotions tend to dominate us, resulting in relative chaos and lack of coordination in our inner lives. A weak-willed person is at the mercy of his own often-irrational emotional urges and impulses.

If, however, we take charge and open our personalities to the leading of the Spirit, a broad range of higher emotions can begin to dominate our inner lives. To be sure, the "natural" emotions continue to occur, but with time we can begin more consciously to guide the overall direction of our emotions. The Spirit can then begin to stabilize and heighten our inner lives.

THE PERSONALITY IN DEATH AND AFTERLIFE

Death occurs when the body can no longer sustain the flow of life energies. One or more of its systems breaks down and the momentum of physical life slows and eventually stops. The mind, because it is linked to the physical brain, also shuts down when the brain dies.

Unlike the mind and body however, the higher parts of personality, the Spirit and soul, do not depend on physical energies for their continued existence. The Spirit is a fragment of God and, as such, continues to exist regardless of what happens to the rest of human personality.

The soul, if it survives in the afterlife, inherits the mind's former function as the conscious center of the personality. The power of will also shifts to the soul after physical death. Whether or not the soul survives physical death depends on the quality of the just-completed human life.

THE SOUL'S SURVIVAL DEPENDS on how full and robust it has grown during the human life. As you may recollect, the mind supplies the raw material of living experience. The Spirit infuses such experience with spiritual values and evolves the soul.

But it is human will that determines the extent of such Spirit influence. If the will has led the personality along a path of active spiritual living, then the soul will be well developed. It will be a storehouse full of spiritual experiences.

If, however, the will ignores or rejects cooperation with the inner Spirit and directs the personality along a largely material course of living, the soul does not have a chance to form and grow strong. When material existence ceases, such a personality, being little more than material, also comes to an end.

Material realities pass away; spiritual realities are eternal. We survive physical death insofar as we identify with the reality of the Father's inner Spirit. Even in the last hours of the human life, if we choose to reach for a relationship with God, we will survive to implement that choice.

THE SPIRIT MAINTAINS a supportive, guiding relationship to the newly surviving soul in the afterlife. And such supportive interaction marks the mere beginnings of an astounding Creator-creature partnership of eternal adventure and growth. The finite human will has determined by virtue of the combined choices of a lifetime to pursue the never-ending search for the Will of the infinite God.

SUMMARY—THE UNIFIED PERSONALITY

The healthy personality is unified; each part fulfills its role in the smoothly working whole. The body provides a stable vehicle for moving through life. The mind is the coordinating center of awareness. The Spirit is the perfect teacher-guide. The soul is the evolving higher self of afterlife potential.

It is by will that we unify our personalities. And it is the inner Spirit-fragment around which our personalities must be unified. The central goal of life is increasingly to act in harmony with the Spirit's leading.

Insofar as we accomplish this goal, our personalities benefit. Our bodies and minds become stable and productive and our souls accumulate spiritual substance. Our entire personalities gain direction and purpose. When such unification occurs, life becomes deeply fulfilling.

UP TO THIS POINT we have considered primarily the nature and function of the isolated personality. But the most profound joys of human existence come from loving and being loved; and love only occurs between individuals.

Loving relationships with other personalities are the gems in the crown of spiritual achievement. We have already touched upon our relationship with the Father's inner Spirit. In the chapters of Part II we shall explore in greater depth the nature of this amazing relationship with the Father, as well as the wonderful potentials inherent in loving relations with other people.

PART II

Relationship:
The Sharing of Personalities

Introduction to Part II

ONE OF THE MOST valuable aspects of our personalities is their innate ability to relate intimately to other personalities. Relationships between personalities do not need to serve some additional separate purpose. They are valuable, enjoyable, and worthwhile in and of themselves.

We experience deep satisfaction as a result of sharing perspectives and feelings with other people. The joy of loving and being loved by another person is the deepest reason for getting involved in a relationship. Personality relationship is its own greatest reward. It is within loving relationships that we make spiritual truths come alive.

If it is true that human relationships are rewarding, then the rewards of the loving relationship we can have with God are so fulfilling as to totally transform our lives. Such a relationship has infinite potentials for growth. There are no limits to the love that God and man can have for each other.

This superb inner friendship serves as the model for all other relationships. In learning to love other people, we reach for the ideal represented by the Father's love for us.

From the depths of our relationship with the Father, a new realization eventually begins to dawn. All human beings are God's spiritual children. We all share common spiritual parentage; the Father has created each of our personalities. Thus we are all brothers and sisters, part of one spiritual family.

EACH OF US IS equally loved by God. When once we really look at a person as another one of the Father's children, it becomes natural to relate to him or her as a spiritual brother or sister. As such fraternal relationships multiply, the worldwide family of God grows closer to becoming a living reality. The eventual realization of the brotherhood of all mankind beneath the loving Fatherhood of God is the ultimate goal of the ages-long process of planetary evolution.

CHAPTER

4

Between God and Man

The possibility of a loving relationship between God and man is based upon the underlying fact that God is a person. We have, at various times, conceived of God as the Infinite Force, the First Cause, the Ultimate Being, the Ground of Reality, and the Creator of the Universe . Such descriptions are valid; but they should never be allowed to eclipse the primary recognition that God is, above all, the original and perfect Personality.

To think of God as a personality is most certainly *not* to think of Him as a sort of glorified human personality, the proverbial old man with a long white beard floating on the clouds. God is no mere projection of man's personality. Instead, it is man that is a finite projection from out of the depths of the Infinite Personality.

By envisioning the highest qualities of human character, by trying to expand human virtues to the point of absolute perfection, we can just barely begin to glimpse the awesome beauty of the Father's personality. Love, compassion, tolerance, nobility, courage, wisdom, strength, majesty—all these personal qualities and more, when multiplied by infinity, can provide but a shadowy silhouette of the Father's true nature. God is the ultimate and perfect Personality.

43

SINCE GOD IS TRULY a Person, it is possible for each of us to experience a truly personal relationship with Him. We can express ourselves to Him and receive His expression to us. We can love Him and we can each experience how He infinitely loves and values us. We can seek His guidance and to the extent that we are ready to receive it, we can benefit from the wisdom of His Will in our lives. We can experience all the joys of the best of human friendships to a vastly deepened degree within the inner friendship of a relationship with God.

Reading a book about the Swiss Alps or hearing someone describe them is nowhere near as much fun as actually being there in the sun and snow. Similarly, it is not really satisfying merely to know about God, hear Him spoken of, theorize about what He is like, or read about Him in books.

But we do not have to depend on such second-hand sources of information. We are not limited to dealing with God at a distance. We can know God *directly,* person to person, within a real, vital, and living relationship. For the Father has placed a part of Himself, a miraculous fragment of His own infinite nature, within each of us. His inner Spirit works constantly for the establishment of a direct and loving God-man relationship.

GOD WITHIN MAN AND BEYOND HIM

One of the most amazing qualities of the God-man relationship is its dual nature. God is on the one hand the Creator and Upholder of the entire universe, and on the other hand the most intimate inner companion of each human being.

It is as if reality were an almost infinite circle with a tiny dot in the middle; God surrounds the outer edge of this circle of reality, and yet for each of us He is the tiny dot at the center of ourselves. Our relationship with God exists at both these extremes of His divine nature.

We can relate to God as the vast and distant Being that has created all of reality, an all-powerful Deity worthy of total reverence. We feel respect and awe when we contemplate the ultimate power and authority of God and the grandeur of His creation. While properly impressing us with God's greatness, such overwhelming perspectives fail to engender trust and love for God in our hearts.

But God is also the closest and most intimate reality within our personalities. No human being can be as close to us as is the loving Spirit presence of the Father.

Through the experience of coming to know this inner Spirit, we grow to love and trust God. The Spirit presence provides us with the opportunity to know God as more than an omnipotent Power way out beyond us, but even as an all-wise and loving personal Friend within us.

THE SPIRITUAL FATHER-CHILD RELATIONSHIP

The inner intimacy and outer grandeur of God are unified within our experience of God as an all-powerful and loving spiritual Father. God is parental in the largest sense as the Creator of all that exists. But He is also a parent in the more immediate sense of being the Creator of each of our personalities.

HOWEVER, BY FAR THE MOST powerful reason for us to relate to God as our spiritual Father is that the tenor of God's love for each of us most closely resembles the love of a devoted father for his child. The Father loves each human being as if that person were His only child. Each one of us is profoundly valuable to God.

The Father is fully dedicated to our spiritual welfare. He spares no effort to help us grow and mature as we move through life. He is infinitely patient with us, forgiving our errors and weaknesses repeatedly. When we falter, He encourages us to rise up and renew our spiritual efforts.

As would a wise human parent, the Father presents us with sufficient difficulties to challenge us and stimulate our growth. Reaching for spiritual ideals does not lead to a life of ease. Having a relationship with God is not like having influential human friends in high places. Trying to follow the leading of the Father's Spirit demands rigorous decision-making. The Father challenges us to reach for ever higher levels of spiritual accomplishment.

And yet, when we stumble, the Father's compassion knows no bounds. He does not judge us by our failures. He sees deeply into our hearts and knows our innermost spiritual yearnings.

It is by these inner soul motivations that He judges us; not so much by what we accomplish as by what we *yearn* to accomplish.

The Father knows that those human longings that are unattainable in time will be attained in eternity. He loves us for our future potentials as well as for our present achievements.

As a human father provides the physical necessities of life for his children, so the heavenly Father has created a surrounding existence that provides for our spiritual needs. He has created a universe of facts, meanings, and values filled with other personalities, a stimulating environment in which we can grow strong and wise. He has structured a reality for His children that is rich in opportunities for choosing between good and evil, an existence which acts as a catalyst for the growth of our souls.

The fact that God has made Himself available to us at any and all times is further indication of the fatherly nature of His love for us. Whenever we seek His Presence we find Him there within, waiting attentively to inspire us.

GOD IS MORE TO US than simply the Father of all mankind. He is deeply involved in an *individual* relationship with *every one* of His spiritual children. Just as a human father develops a special relationship with each of his children, so our spiritual Father has a unique relationship with each one of us.

Because no human personality is the same as any other, the Father's interaction with each of His children is different. He literally knows every single one of us as a true individual, and loves us each in a special way. Only an infinite Father could love every one of the children in His family equally as His favorite.

The truth that God is our Father is no mere concept or metaphor. The unutterable satisfactions of loving God as a Father and being loved by Him are *real,* and they are available to any of us who open our hearts to receive Him.

There is no joy like that of the mortal child who has found the universal Father and knows himself to have a special place in the Father's family. Such a human child has found the one Person who is worthy to receive that child's total loyalty and adoration. And to be able to give such unstinted adulation in worshipful recognition of the Father's matchless and perfect nature is the culminating fulfillment of human personality.

FAITH: ENTERING THE GOD-MAN RELATIONSHIP

The Father never forces Himself on a human being. Having given us free will, God respects our authority to shape the course of our own lives even if we choose to shut the Father out of our lives. The only way that a relationship between us and God can occur is if we willfully choose to initiate it. We do not blindly stumble upon a relationship with the Father. If we are *actively looking* for God we will find Him.

If we are not actively looking for God, we will not be aware that God exists. The Father reveals Himself to those who sincerely search for such inner revelation. The only prerequisite to a relationship with God is the desire to know Him. It is within such a context of desire for God that faith is born.

It is like taking a seed that has long been dormant and placing it in fertile earth and keeping it well watered. Soon it sprouts and begins to grow. Similarly, when the dormant seed of faith is planted within a deep desire to know God, then the conditions are right for such a faith-seed to sprout and grow strong.

FAITH IS THE DOOR through which we approach a relationship with God. In order to know and love the Father we must faith-recognize the Father's existence. But how can we gain such faith in the first place?

At first, having faith is like taking a step out into the unknown. Initially we do not know God because we have had no previous experience with Him. So the first small bit of faith must be a leap out into what is not yet known. It means having trust in a reality that we are not quite sure is there. In a sense, a person starting out on the faith adventure says, "I am not sure that God exists, but if He does, I very much want to know Him."

Having initial faith is similar to what a scientist does when he starts an experiment with a hypothesis, a sort of educated guess. For instance, he might start with the hypothesis that dripping water can wear away rock. He is not sure that the hypothesis is true, but he starts with the assumption that it *is* true, and then performs experiments to see if reality supports his assumption. He proceeds to drip a lot of water on a rock. After a while he can conclude through the results of such experiments whether or not his hypothesis is in fact supported by reality.

Similarly, we can start off with the faith-assumption that God exists and can experiment with a relationship with Him based on that assumption. After a while our experiences will begin to support the reality of the inner Presence of the Father. Our faith-hypothesis will be confirmed by such experiential evidence.

But we must start this confirmation process with an initial particle of faith. A raindrop may form high up in a cloud when water vapor starts to collect around a tiny particle of dust floating in the air. Similarly, we need faith as the spiritual "particle" around which God-confirming experience can gather. And each such confirming spiritual experience adds to the fullness of our faith.

A POWERFUL FACTOR IN such initial faith steps is the fact that the inner Spirit is actually present within our personalities and is ever alert to even the faintest flickers of faith. The Spirit-fragment attempts constantly to fan such initial faith-sparks into a steady flame which can eventually grow bright and powerful within our souls.

THE FAITH OF A HUMAN BEING in the heavenly Father resembles the total trust that a young child naturally gives to a devoted parent. But such child-like spiritual faith in God is, nevertheless, quite consistent with the fully developed intellectual and emotional life of an adult personality.

FAITH IN GOD GROWS much as does trust in a human relationship. When we first meet another person we do not know him at all. At first we put a tiny bit of trust out to this new acquaintance and wait to see the kind of response we get to such tentative friendship.

If the trust is respected and we are given trust and affection in return, we feel secure in giving even more of ourselves to this new friend. Eventually trust and love build on both sides of the relationship to the point where a full and enduring friendship exists.

This same growth sequence occurs in a relationship with the Father. At first we put only a small bit of our faith forward. After all, we do not yet know God very well. As in a human relationship, without such an initial venture of trust the relationship would never begin.

As we increasingly experience God's love for us and learn of the tremendous trustworthiness of the Father, we place ever larger amounts of our faith and love into the relationship. Soon our spiritual faith-certitude, based on accumulating experience, becomes virtually unshakeable. When we have developed such full faith we know that the one reality in life of which we can be most assured is our continuing relationship with the Father. Such faith is the entryway to an eternal partnership between ourselves and God. It is the first fledgling step that we take on what will be a never-ending voyage of discovery into the depths of the infinite nature of the universal Father.

COMMUNION: HOW GOD AND MAN COMMUNICATE

The heart of our relationship with God lies in the process of *communion*. Communion, in the broader sense of the term, refers to that subtle and mysterious process by which God and man share each with the other. Communion is *commun*ication that results in spiritual *union* between God and man. It is through this experience of inner communion that we come to know God more fully.

Just as there are many different ways to communicate in a human relationship, communion with God can likewise take many different forms. Meditation, prayer, and worship are all terms that have been used to describe the many subtle shadings of spiritual communion.

COMMUNION OCCURS IN TWO directions: we expressing ourselves to God, and God expressing Himself to us.

In communion we share our inner yearnings with God, our hopes and fears, our daily failures and triumphs, the dilemmas which we face. We ask for help in the ongoing struggles of life and give thanks for what the Father has already provided.

Although most people use words when communing with God, the inner Spirit picks up the feelings we have that lie too deep for verbal expression. God has no need of words; He senses the true attitude of our souls directly and fully from within.

In sharing with God, it is best for us to express ourselves in the manner that is most natural and spontaneous for us. The Father does not require specialized procedures and formal codewords in order to hear us. He is fully capable of understanding us when we express ourselves to Him in the way in which we are most comfortable. He inevitably understands the real meanings which underlie the words and concepts we use. With a little bit of practice our expression to the Father can become fully free flowing and very enjoyable.

Similarly, it often takes some practice before we can become effective at discerning the Father's expression to us. We must willfully train ourselves to become skillful at receiving the inspiration of the Spirit. We must learn how to open our minds and direct our awareness Godward.

To receive inner inspiration we have to try to cultivate a combination of two qualities of thinking. We have to be focused and yet spontaneous, attentive and yet free-flowing.

It's like a river flowing within its banks. The banks keep the water moving in a certain direction. But within those banks the water is free to swirl spontaneously. We have to keep our thoughts directed in a generally spiritual direction, and yet leave them flexible enough to be influenced and guided by the inner Spirit.

If we don't channel our thoughts enough, they go wandering off to things like bills to be paid and what's on T.V. But if we guide our thoughts too much, then our old patterns of thinking dominate and we leave no room for the new insights of the Spirit to enter in.

One way to reach for inspiration from the Spirit is to assume an attitude of intense inner listening. Suppose you had lost a little kitten up in the attic of your house and you were standing in the half dark, listening intently for its frightened mewing, trying to determine where it was. You would be highly focused and attentive.

Similarly we can be inwardly focused and attentive, "listening" for new insights from the Spirit. We can eagerly watch the flow of our thoughts for the appearance of original strands of inspiration. Once we recognize such new truths, we can carefully evaluate them and integrate them into our lives in a balanced way.

But we rarely develop sensitivity to the Spirit's leading suddenly or dramatically. Such sensitivity is the result of our persistent and stable efforts to know and do the Father's Will. It usually does not result from the cultivation of extreme or trance-like states of mind. Real receptivity to the inner Spirit's leading is the natural result of our desire to love the Father and grow closer to Him. True communion with God results in a balanced, fruitful, and love-dominated life.

QUALITIES OF THE GOD-MAN RELATIONSHIP

We can depend on God absolutely. He will never betray our trust in Him. He unfailingly does what is best for His human children, what is in our eternal long-term interest. Sometimes His Will for us requires struggle and effort, but regardless of such difficulties, living with God leads to progressive fulfillment. The Father will never let us down. The more relevant question is how dependably loyal are we to God. That is what determines the growth of the God-man relationship.

Regardless of how far we may stray from the leading of His Spirit, God never gives up on us. The God-man relationship grows dim only when we give up on God. The Father never ceases His efforts to reach one of us if we are spiritually lost. No matter what we have done, the Father will accept and forgive us if we sincerely seek a renewal of our relationship with Him.

There is no negative factor of history or environment that can block God from reaching us if we desire such contact. As regards the opportunity to get to know the Father, it is literally true that all men are created equal.

HUMAN NATURE COMES complete with an inbuilt sense of curiosity, a thirst for new and challenging situations. Such a discovery urge is constantly being fulfilled in our relations with the Father. We need never fear that our relationship with God will become dull or boring. Just when life seems to have become a bit settled and repetitive, the Father stimulates us with demanding situations in the outer life, or generates new spiritual ideals to reach for in the inner life.

Because God is infinite, there will always remain vast areas of His nature that we have not yet explored. Regardless of how well we know Him, enticing mysteries will remain to draw us eagerly on into deeper love and involvement with Him. The spiritual life is not static and lulling; it is a thrilling and dynamic search.

EACH OF US YEARNS for someone who fully loves and understands and respects us, someone who really knows what is going on inside of us and cares about what happens to us, someone who needs and appreciates us and is genuinely glad that we exist.

And each of us likewise needs someone whom we can care for without reservation and trust with our innermost secrets, someone whom we can idolize and serve, knowing that such a person is worthy to receive our total loyalty, someone whom we fully respect and admire, who deserves every last bit of the love that we can give. Each of us yearns in the depths of our being thus to love and be loved.

Many of us search in vain for a human relationship to fulfill these longings. We fail to realize that no mere human being can love us totally or deserves to be loved by us totally. Time and again we are frustrated, because we seek perfection in imperfect human relationships. A human parent, spouse, or friend cannot but fail to meet such expectations.

Only a perfect Person can love us perfectly, and only a perfect Person is worthy to receive our gift of total love and loyalty. And only when we enter into a relationship with God, will we experience the true and lasting fulfillment of these yearnings which lie in the innermost depths of our souls.

CHAPTER

5

Human Relationships

THE NEED FOR HUMAN RELATIONSHIPS

Human relationships are essential for the normal functioning of our personalities. The need for interaction with other people is built into the very fiber of human nature. Loving fellowship somehow provides an essential nutrient without which our personalities deteriorate. It has long been recognized that prolonged isolation from human contact has a disastrous effect on man's psyche.

When we isolate ourselves from the balancing influence of ongoing friendships, we tend increasingly to swing to extremes of mood and behavior. Under such conditions spiritual experience, if it occurs at all, often becomes fanatical and bizarre. Happiness fades as the mental life grows inbred and stagnant from lack of interpersonal stimulation.

When we cut ourselves off from our fellows, our conclusions become skewed. We begin to look at life from a distorted angle. Our isolation sends us drifting out toward the edge of reality. Our views of ourselves, other people, and the world in general become misaligned, out of focus.

Ongoing human relationships are crucial in that they broaden and balance us. When we can share our experiences with others, life's high times are enhanced; they become more enjoyable through the sharing. And when we feel the cutting edge of sorrow our hardship is softened and made bearable by the supportive sympathy of caring companions.

Through appreciating the inner motivations and outer lives of those around us we avoid becoming narrow and self-centered. By understanding what is important to other people we broaden our own ideals. Such sharing provides comparisons that help us branch out beyond our own conclusions. A balanced and broad appreciation of life is best obtained when we have continuous contact with other peoples' viewpoints.

Both for the sake of ourselves and for the sake of humankind, we cannot afford to isolate ourselves from others. The fate of the individual is intertwined with the future of all humanity. This essential interconnection of man and mankind is powerfully portrayed by the seventeenth century poet, John Donne.

> No man is an iland, intire of it selfe;
> every man is a peece of the Continent,
> a part of the maine; if a Clod be washed away
> by the Sea, Europe is the lesse, as well as if a
> Promontorie were, as well as if a Mannor of thy friends
> or of thine owne were; any mans death diminishes me,
> because I am involved in Mankinde:
> And therefore never send to know for whom the bell tolls;
> It tolls for thee.[1]

THE REWARDS OF RELATIONSHIP

The give and take of relationships tends to knock the rough edges off the individual human personality. It is interesting to note that when a jeweler wishes to bring out the beauty of a raw semi-precious stone he places it in a tumbler along with a number of other stones. As the stones revolve and grate upon each other within the rotating chamber, their rough outer edges begin to chip and flake off. And as the process continues hour after hour the stones become increasingly smooth and round, until their mutual scouring action results in

---

[1] John Donne (1572–1631), *The Complete Poetry and Selected Prose of John Donne and the Complete Poetry of William Blake,* New York, Random House, 1941, P. 332

each stone having a shining surface which displays its natural inner beauty.

An active life of relating to a variety of people has a similar polishing effect on human personality. Early in life the personality is abrasive, egoistic and immature. As it increasingly interacts with other personalities in the rough and tumble of life, its raw edges are worn away and the individual gains compatibility with others. Such interactions bring out the beautiful inner potentials of the personality. They polish its surface to a transparent shine that allows these inner beauties to show through.

Human relationships are the living laboratory within which we mature. Without the stimulation and challenge of personal interaction, our personalities would never develop. The give and take of the social arena demands that we integrate our personal desires with the desires of the other personalities around us.

In response to such demands we can develop many desirable qualities. We can become tolerant, altruistic, self-disciplined, and wise as we learn to harmonize our wants with the wants of others.

Goodness and unselfishness can only be practiced within relationships. And love, the master spiritual emotion, must be shared between two or more personalities. Relationships provide the opportunity to grow in ways that are exquisitely rewarding.

AN ACTIVE SPIRITUAL life and the formation of healthy human relationships reinforce each other. When we gain spiritual inspiration and strength from God, our human relationships prosper. And loving human relationships, in turn, mightily spur our spiritual progress, yielding a rich harvest of new insights for our souls.

THE FATHER'S SPIRITUAL FAMILY

The brotherhood of man is more than simply a humanistic ideal; it is based on the underlying fact that each of us is a child of God. What makes two people brother and sister is that they were born of and reared by the same parents. To say that God is a common spiritual Parent to every man and woman, to say that we are all His children, is to acknowledge that in its very essence ours is a familial relationship. We really are brothers and sisters in the Father's spiritual family.

When we recognize that we all share the same divine Source and can anticipate a similar thrilling destiny, a profound sense of comradeship begins to grow between us. As we progressively realize that we each have God's Spirit within us, and that we are each similarly reaching inward for a relationship with the Father, our relationships with each other take on a quality of tremendous adventure shared between friends. Such a common bond brings us closer together. We actually begin to love other people as part of our own intimate family group.

When it finally dawns on us just how much the Father loves us, we naturally seek in some way to show our appreciation for such love. What can we offer to Him? Few gifts please the Father more than to see His many children relating to each other with real fraternal affection. Any parent is naturally pleased to see his children treat each other with loving consideration. To love other people as our brothers and sisters is a validation and completion of the Father's love for us.

The God-man relationship is the flowing source of brotherly love. In loving our fellows we attempt in our own small human way to channel to others some of the divine love that the Father showers on us. Ultimately, what we are reaching for is to be able to love our fellows with the compassion and wisdom that is typical of the way God loves us.

IT ISN'T ENOUGH simply to agree that we're all part of one big family; we must actually try to treat each other as we would a favorite brother or sister. As long as the family of God remains a mere intellectual belief, it cannot transform peoples' relations with each other. The ideal of brotherhood must be translated into an actual way of living. *Loving actions* are the fruit that spiritual brotherhood must bear if it is to become a meaningful reality.

Coming to know and love our fellows is a tremendously enriching process. But it does indeed require dedication, persistent efforts at understanding and tolerance. It is when your next door neighbor's barking dog has just awakened you for the third time in one night that the challenge presents itself. At such times brotherly affection does not come easily.

In order to love others despite their shortcomings we must gain patience, strength, and perspective from our inner relationship with God. We can learn the self-control that is crucial to applied loving from the inner Spirit. By taking our relationship cues from the Father we grow in our ability to truly love each other as brothers and sisters in His family.

IMPROVING RELATIONSHIPS

The key to improving human relationships lies in inviting the Father to participate in them. We can know how best to relate to our fellows by consulting the inner Spirit, by communing with God right in the very midst of interacting with another person.

When we thus consult God, we draw upon resources that go far beyond our human capabilities. We are not dependent upon what other people say, or what the situation seems to indicate, or what past experience would suggest. We have access to the Father's perfect assessment of what should be done in that particular relationship situation.

Insofar as we tap this higher resource and act upon its inspiration, we are able to respond in startlingly powerful ways to the challenges inherent in human relationships. We harness spiritual energies of a higher order to transform them. By importing advanced spiritual technology into the relatively backward realm of human interaction, we can learn the self-control that is crucial to applied loving.

When the love-source we are tapping is infinite, our ability to uplift finite relationships takes a dimensional leap forward. We progress markedly in our ability to treat others in the way that God would have us treat them.

As an example of such spiritualizing of relationships, suppose a friend of yours was in an irritable mood and told you to go jump in the lake. You could respond to him in one of two ways. If you depended solely on your human tendencies, you would probably become angry and send a few choice words back his way. If, however, you had developed the habit of sharing inwardly with the Father in the midst of your human interactions, you would be able to delay your angry reaction momentarily while you sought Spirit inspiration.

Through such communion you would gain self-control and perspective on the situation. You would get a flash of insight as to how the Father was seeing your friend at that instant and what you might do to resolve the situation compassionately. You would recollect the ongoing love you have for your friend and would gather strength to come from that foundation of love in your reaction to him.

When you did speak, you would be taking your cues from the inner Spirit rather than from your upset friend or the aggravating situation. Rather than being brought down to the level of your friend's irritability, you would come from a higher place and use spiritual leverage to lift him lovingly to a level of greater calm and broadened perspective. Such a spiritually inspired reaction would strikingly improve the continuing relationship between the two of you.

A MARKED IMPROVEMENT in relationships occurs when we begin to have faith in our fellows in the way that the Father has faith in us. God certainly sees our imperfections, but He always gives us the benefit of the doubt. He always relates to us with the expectation that we will live up to our higher potentials. If we are truly trying to treat others as the Father treats us, then we relate primarily to their actual accomplishments and potential achievements. We see them in the best light, and support and encourage them.

Having faith in people means helping them have faith in themselves. We respect them and expect them eventually to live up to their own highest ideals. It means focusing on their growth in the future rather than on their lack of growth in the past. Showing faith in others always adds to them; it never takes anything away. It ever looks for and encourages the best in another's nature.

FORGIVENESS: THE HEALING OF RELATIONSHIPS

Human beings are not perfect. They will always be making mistakes, and will even at times act with conscious evil intent. Imperfection is a part of human nature. And many times such actions result in one person more or less willfully wronging another.

It is crucial to both the health of the individual personality and to the quality of human relationships, that we develop the ability to forgive our fellows when such wrongdoing occurs. The accumulation of resentments and the buildup of the urge to revenge are some of the most destructive tendencies which we can allow ourselves to fall into.

It is most important that we develop the spiritual habit of cleansing our personalities of such emotional toxins soon after we begin to experience them. Prolonged resentments destroy relationships and rob life of fulfillment. We must counter such tendencies by cultivating the ability to forgive.

Forgiveness is an inner process of cooperation with the Spirit in which we sincerely attempt to understand another person's motives and actions. When someone has wronged us, if we can understand how he was feeling and what moved him to act as he did, we have a better chance of sincerely forgiving his wrongdoing.

When we forgive, the spiritual power of love for another person vanquishes our natural tendencies to resent being wronged. Resentment is self-centered; it is rooted in our own wounded feelings. When we seek communion with the Father and pray for wisdom to overcome our resentment, our focus enlarges beyond a primary concern with ourselves. We become more concerned with doing the Father's Will, with doing what is right in the situation. When we pray to be able to forgive, our outlook expands beyond ourselves to include compassion for the person that has wronged us.

WE HAVE THE PERFECT model of forgiveness to imitate when we look at how often and how fully the Father forgives us when we do wrong. He totally understands; He knows perfectly what goes on within us when we backslide. And each time we slip He forgives us fully. His love for us never lets up for an instant. It is our privilege to attempt to bring some of that divine forgiving quality into our human relationships.

Interestingly enough, it is likely that we experience the Father's forgiveness of us more when we in turn forgive our fellow human beings. For instance, when we have forgiven someone who has lied to us, it is easier for us to accept the fact that the Father forgives us when we have been dishonest. When we forgive others we become increasingly aware of the very nature of forgiveness itself. As a result of this heightened sensitivity to the experience of forgiving, we are better able to understand how the Father can so lovingly and fully forgive us.

As we mature spiritually and are more influenced by the Spirit's inner leading, we become adept at conducting relationships along harmonious lines. We learn to resolve interpersonal crises through the healing power of forgiveness.

APPLYING LOVE THROUGH SERVICE

The medium of love in relationships is service, doing for others what we sense they want done, and what is ultimately beneficial for them. When we experience the overflow of the Father's love within our souls, it is natural that we seek outlets for such abundance in channels of loving service to our fellows. Finding avenues of service is one of the most powerful urges of the spiritually maturing personality.

The devoted mother gives to her child with gladness. Giving freely of ourselves to others is a tonic to the soul and has an invigorating influence upon the entire personality. It is a joyous expression of the amazing fact that God has given us much more than we need, enough for us to give richly to those around us. Rendering of loving service ranks among the most fulfilling of personality functions.

When we understand how much God is doing for us, we begin to feel a real yearning to find ways similarly to do things for other people; the Father's generosity is tremendously contagious. We begin to realize that the highest form of service to God is service to the other children in His family. We reach the overwhelming conclusion that the only right way to use the blessings we have been given is to share them.

OF THE MANY CHANNELS of service that we can develop, the spiritual service of sharing God with others is by far the most fulfilling. When we have found the Father and experienced the unparalleled satisfactions of a living relationship with Him, it becomes the greatest service-joy to share the sumptuous feast that He has prepared for us with those who are as yet spiritually hungry.

There is no more important service than that of introducing a searching individual to the rewards of the spiritual life. To assist the Father in awakening our brothers and sisters to His Presence within them is to work in a service-partnership with God that is truly sublime.

∽∽∽

CHAPTER

6

Love:
The Cornerstone of
Relationship

THE NATURE OF LOVE

Love is essential to relationships. Without love our relationships would be dead and cold. Sincere affection is the lifeblood, the flowing vital substance of our interactions with both God and our fellow men.

This fundamental force of love is the spiritual web which binds God's far-flung family together. We are not isolated cosmic orphans, but loved and loving members of the Father's family. Love lends transcendent meaning to our existence.

The foremost quality of God's nature is His all-encompassing love. All other qualities, such as His justice, power, and wisdom, are blended into the Father's caring for us: but it is His love that is preeminent. Divine affection is the unshakeable foundation upon which our relationship with God rests. And to the extent that we take in the Father's love and give it out to our fellows, it likewise becomes the cornerstone of our human relationships.

Loving is the central progressive activity of the spiritual life. The best indicator of our inner growth is the extent to which we love God and love other people. No real spiritual progress can occur unless we progress in our ability to love. Our overall personality development closely parallels the expansion of our powers of affection. In fact, our entire human civilization matures only insofar as loving relations between individuals begin to dominate in the affairs of men.

It is noteworthy that when asked what a person should do to gain eternal life, that master spiritual teacher, Jesus of Nazareth, responded simply and directly that man should *love* God with all his heart, mind, soul, and strength, and should *love* his neighbor as himself. The spiritual wisdom of the ages lies folded within that statement, waiting to be unfurled within the heart of the person who searches for living truth.

The love of God and the love of man mightily reinforce each other. Some may feel that love for our fellows grows as a result of the inner love of the God-man relationship. Others might claim that we first experience love in human relationships and only later do we learn to love the Father.

Actually, it is accurate to think of love as originating in both our inner and outer lives simultaneously; love for God and love for people are two necessary sides of the same spiritual coin. Within the experience of loving and being loved by God, we learn lessons that are invaluable in our attempts to love our fellow man. And as we experience loving our spiritual brothers and sisters, we circle back and even further deepen our appreciation of the Father's love.

UNFORTUNATELY, THE WORD "love" has been used rather indiscriminately to describe qualities of relationship that are not at all loving. This practice has caused much confusion. Too often people say "I love you" when they actually mean "I need you." Too often they claim love as the motive when what they are actually trying to do is make another person fulfill their own needs.

This is not real love. Genuine love does not constantly take from another person; it gives to the one who is loved. It encourages freedom and strength in another, rather than fostering dependence and weakness.

True love is an excess, an abundance of affection. False love is the result of a deficiency of affection; it selfishly seeks love to fill its own void. It is indeed ironic and tragic that such crippled and crippling attitudes have been justified time and again by the claim that they are born of "love."

SPIRITUAL LOVE CANNOT abide peaceably alongside hatred. When we love we are not satisfied merely to ignore hatred. We attempt literally to dissolve it, to transform it into love both within ourselves and within other people.

Love acts like the microscopic antibodies that fight disease in our bodies. When they encounter germs they don't just float on by; they instinctively attack and destroy such dangerous microbes. Likewise, genuine love does not react passively when it encounters hostility. It dissipates and conquers the negative emotions that it encounters.

Spiritual love takes the initiative in relationships. Love is aggressive in reaching out to others. When our souls are filled with the Father's love, we can courageously approach and smother hatred by daring to act lovingly even in the face of the unloving actions of a misguided brother or sister. When our love is truly rooted in God, there is no negative emotion we can encounter that is strong enough to overpower our transforming affection.

AT ONE TIME OR ANOTHER, most of us have experienced anger with people who have wronged us. We want to make them treat us with more respect. What we fail to understand is that the best way to get someone to respect and love us is to love them first.

It's not that we're trying to conquer other people with love. When two people have come to love each other neither one of them must conquer the other because love has conquered them both. They have both consented to settle their disputes according to the higher authority of love.

LOYALTY IS ONE OF the qualities that can always be found alongside genuine love. Loyalty implies a stable and far-reaching dedication toward the support of the person or principle that is loved.

For instance, if we deeply love truth we are unfailingly loyal to it. The loyal devotion of the inner Spirit-fragments is utterly dependable precisely because their love for us is boundless. As we grow increasingly to love our brothers and sisters, our dedication to their welfare becomes more strong and steady; we become more loyal friends to them.

As our love for the Father blossoms, we evolve a profound form of loyalty to God. In coming to know the Father, we arrive at the inescapable conclusion that here is a Person who deserves our total dedication. Here is a Leader who can be fully trusted. Here at last is a Mentor in whom we have such complete faith that we can safely guide our entire lives by His counsel. Our love for God eventually results in a replete sense of loyalty, a pervasive dedication to knowing and doing His Will.

AND LOVE IS ever active. True love cannot remain a mere inner ideal. When we feel genuine spiritual affection we will always find ways to convey our love to others. Love makes itself known; it results in changed relationships. The ever-present challenge is to find new and more potent ways to give service-expression to our love for God and man.

THE GIVE AND TAKE OF LOVE

The very essence of love is that it is a dynamic process between personalities. It can never be a static possession, a sort of buried treasure hoarded in our souls. We cannot keep love to ourselves; it must be *shared* in order to be *real*.

It's like water flowing into a garden hose. The only way that water can continue to flow into one end of the hose is for water to simultaneously pour out the other end.

The only way that we can receive the Father's love is if we are simultaneously pouring our love out to our fellows. As we pour out our love, we make room in our hearts to receive more of it from the Father. If we keep our love bottled up inside it only becomes stale and unreal.

One of the identifying marks of real spiritual love is that it is freely given. Valid love does not ask anything in return, because it contains its own greatest reward; the process of loving is inherently satisfying. The fact that it feels good to love is that much more reason for doing it.

Real love can be freely given because the supply never runs out. Love flows from God, a spiritual source that is inexhaustible. In fact, the more we use it, the more there is to use. Imagine how surprised we'd be if each time we spent a hundred dollars, we got two hundred dollars back. Money spent is usually money gone. The economics of love, however, are strangely reversed; the more of it we spend, the more of it we have.

We do not lose love when we give it away. On the contrary, it is only by giving it away that we can gain it as a personal experience. It is when we love another person that we most vividly feel the flow of love. The experience of loving is at least as rewarding as the experience of being loved.

THE NEED TO RECEIVE love has been the focus of much psychological research. What has been largely overlooked, however, is that for the health of our personalities it is as crucial for us to be able to *give* love to others as it is for us to receive it from them.

The urge to express love, to be loving, is a primal force within us. We experience extreme frustration when we are unable spontaneously and authentically to express affection to our fellows.

Unfortunately, to some degree, all of us experience blockages in our ability to be fully loving. It takes courage to release ourselves in love-giving. There are natural fears and inhibitions we must overcome.

In order to give love to others, we need to feel that we ourselves are loved. Loving is a natural response to the experience of being loved. At first our ability to love others is conditioned by whether they are loving us back. If for some reason they are not able to return our love, we feel rejected and our ability to love falters.

But when we grow close to God we feel loved all the time. We are constantly nourished and replenished by His love. We no longer have to depend on other peoples' love; we experience a surplus of love from God. This abundance of love from the Father liberates us to love others without holding back. We can give our love freely even if, for the time being, others are unable to love us in return.

IT IS TRAGICALLY TRUE that the most difficult type of individual for people to love is the person who himself is unable to love. A vicious cycle develops. The person is unloving. Other people don't like being around him and they don't give him love. He feels rejected and becomes bitter and even less loving than before, at which point people reject him even more. He just keeps getting more isolated and more unloving as time goes on.

Ironically, such an unloving person is exactly the individual who most needs our love. His situation is desperate. Because at first he cannot love in return, few people are willing to give him the love he needs. Only if we are spiritually active are we likely to be able to love him. That's because we are not dependent on his loving us; our source of love is God. We are able to love him even if he is unloving to us.

As he soaks up our unconditional love his personality can begin to thaw and he can break the vicious circle of isolation. He sees that other people can, in fact, love him. He starts to feel better about himself, and then he can begin to love other people once more.

There is another way for such an unloving person to begin to love again. At any time he has the opportunity to open his heart to the love of God. The Father's affection will always be there for him, regardless of how unlovable he may think he has become. It is simply a matter of his opening himself to receive it.

If he will allow himself to experience how much the Father loves him he will naturally begin to love the Father in return. From there he can turn to his fellows, and begin the slow but thorough transformation of his human relationships by the inner power of love.

WHILE SOME OF US have a problem giving love, others find it more difficult to accept love when it is being offered. This often happens when we feel, for some reason, that we are not worthy of being loved.

In Chapter 9 we will explore this issue of self-esteem in greater depth. But for now it is important to recognize that when we gladly accept other peoples' love, our relationships prosper. When we obviously rejoice in receiving the love of our fellows, they feel that their love is valued and they are encouraged to continue loving us.

It is even more important that we allow ourselves to receive God's love. Again the problem that often arises is that sometimes we feel unworthy to receive the Father's love; we just cannot understand how God could really care about us. But it *is true!* We *are* totally supported and surrounded by His love. And we can experience that life-changing affection by simply opening our hearts in faith and allowing the Father's love to fill us.

WHEN OUR PERSONALITIES are spiritually developed, we become well versed in the give and take of love. We experience the inner ecstasy of receiving the Father's perfect love and the joy of loyally loving God in return. And we rejoice in the overflow of such affection into our human relationships.

THE GROWTH OF LOVE

We can willfully increase both the quantity and quality of our love. We can love more of the people around us and can develop a wiser type of affection for our fellows.

Our appreciation for fine music grows as we listen to it more often. Similarly, our understanding of the nature of love grows as we love people more often.

With time, we can make spiritual affection the dominant emotion in our lives. The light of love grows so full and constant that all lesser emotions recede in relative shadow. Negative emotions are dissolved by the steady stream of love that comes to pervade our relationships. We actually begin to live according to love.

LOVE DOES NOT GROW by itself; we must apply ourselves to develop it. A ballerina spends many years of dedicated effort mastering her art. We must dedicate ourselves to learning the ways of love from the inner Spirit. With practice we can increasingly develop the habit of giving affection. When we have thus trained ourselves in the habit of love it becomes second nature for us to share it as we move through life. It flows naturally from us.

As we apply ourselves, we develop our own personal methods of increasing our ability to love. We learn how to mold our unique temperaments so as to increase our powers of affection.

THE MOST IMPORTANT ELEMENT in our growing to love our fellows is that we come to understand them. Misunderstanding of another's motives usually leads to antagonism. If we are having a hard time liking someone, the most effective thing we can do is attempt to understand deeply why this person is acting the way he is.

Sincere prayer to understand other people and to be able to love them has a powerful effect on our personalities. It makes us more tolerant and supportive of the unique position they may be in. By trying to put ourselves in their shoes we understand how they feel.

When we thus understand our fellows, our affection for them tends to dominate naturally over more negative feelings.

We cannot simply love someone with a snap of the fingers. Love grows over time and as a result of our persistent desire to be loving.

LOVING WISELY

With time the *quality* of our love can also improve. We learn not only to love more, but to love more wisely. When love is not tempered by wisdom it can be most destructive. Examples of unwise love include the overindulgent love of a parent who spoils a child, and the dependent love that a weak man or woman feels toward a domineering spouse. Such unwise love relationships distort the personalities of those who are involved in them.

THERE ARE MANY ELEMENTS that contribute to wise love. For example, it is balanced; it does not swing to extremes. When two wise people love each other, the temporary tensions of daily living do not rock the underlying stability of their affection for each other.

Wisdom implies that we love in ways that work toward the long-term growth of the person whom we are loving, rather than simply providing him with short-term pleasure. Sometimes the wise parent must discipline his child out of loving concern for the child's long-term betterment even though such discipline is unpleasant for the child in the immediate situation.

When we love wisely we are tactful. For instance, the wise husband who wants to inform his wife that she tends to dominate conversations, does so with great sensitivity and a lot of personal support.

Wise love is well-informed. The wise parent is constantly looking for new information and experience that will help him love his children in more healthy ways. Wise love results from absorbing truth wherever it is found and applying it within relationships.

As usual, we find the perfect model of wise loving in God's love for us. If we are ever in doubt as to how to love wisely, we can always ask the Father for inspiration. If we ask persistently, His inner Spirit will unfailingly show us how to most effectively love our fellows.

Our love becomes wise insofar as we try to live out the highest values of truth, beauty, and goodness. Wise love is true. It never tries to hide reality from the one who is loved. It is straightforward and whole, courageous and always dependable. Genuine love is also beautiful; it glows with an inner purity that is truly inspiring. And wise love is always good; it ever seeks to do what is best for the one who is loved.

THE GROWTH OF LOVE need never end. Always will there be new vistas of the Father's affection opening up before us; always shall we be striving to live up to our expanding understanding of His divine love.

CHAPTER

7

Family:
The Seed-Bed of
Relationship

THE QUALITY OF FAMILY LIFE has a strong impact on both the healthy development of our individual personalities and the overall stability of a civilization. Each family unit is a vital link in the cultural chain that reaches back into the distant past and forward into the unformed future. By providing the maturing child with the accumulated culture of previous generations, the family lends continuity to the slow evolution of civilization.

If the family life of any society is unstable the growth of that society is gravely endangered. As family life deteriorates and the number of poorly adjusted individuals increases, a great strain is placed on the overall resources of society.

The viability of any culture, its ability to survive and grow over time, depends on the strength of its family life. The character of a society and its individual members can only reach as high as the family values it espouses.

MARRIAGE: THE FOUNDATION

The structure of a building is strong only if it rests upon a stable foundation. The structure of family life is strong only if it rests upon the foundation of a stable marriage relationship. While society establishes the general norms of family structure, it is the individual husband and wife who evolve the unique environment within their own family. They determine the atmosphere of the home by the tenor of their relationship.

If they are loving and cooperative they can resolve the characteristic challenges of family life. If, however, they allow antagonism to gain the upper hand in their relationship, they and their children will reap the traumatic harvest of family fragmentation.

CONTRARY TO POPULAR FANTASIES, marriage is not a never-ending wonderland of romantic and sexual fulfillment. Unfortunately, many newlyweds approach marriage with the attitude, "What can I get out of this marriage?" instead of "What can I put into this marriage?"

Surely romantic love is an important part of a new relationship. But a successful marriage contains at least equal parts of struggle, confusion, differences of opinion, and compromise. These are unavoidable realities that result when one human being lives day in and day out with another.

A successful marriage is a working partnership that has been hammered out over time. Husband and wife have evolved effective methods of resolving the differences that naturally arise when two people collaborate on a life-long venture. If young couples could approach marriage with more open-eyed realism and less wide-eyed romanticism, they would be much better prepared to deal with the occasional rough and tumble of married life.

Romantic passion alone will not keep a man and woman together. Only the wise love which springs from spiritual sources and which is applied practically within a daily working partnership can endure and blossom into a marriage of life-long fulfillment.

GENERALLY SPEAKING, MEN AND WOMEN have different psychological strong points. Their views on most things in life tend to reflect these differences between male and female natures. Depending on how a couple deals with such differences in psychological style, they can either be a source of bitter conflict or they can lead the man-woman team to accomplishments that neither one could achieve alone.

For example, it seems that women tend to be more intuitive and men tend to be more logical. Sometimes when a couple disagrees on an issue the woman has an intuitive sense of what is right but has trouble logically explaining why she feels the way she does. The man, on the other hand, can logically justify his stance. However, using his logical abilities he may end up convincing himself of something that he wants to believe even though it might not quite be true. And even though the woman may sense the truth of the matter intuitively she cannot get around the logical certainty of the man.

If the man and woman use their respective strengths to combat each other, they both become frustrated and antagonistic and they never resolve their disagreement. The man thinks the woman is being emotional and illogical, and the woman thinks the man is being insensitive and insincere.

However, if they can learn to trust each other they can each use their strengths to resolve the issue cooperatively. The woman intuitively senses the essential nature of the problem. The man respects her intuition and makes an effort to understand logically why she feels the way she does. Once he understands, he can help her to explain her position logically, and together they can work out a resolution to the problem.

Working together, the man and woman can both intuitively know and logically understand what is right. They can look at the problem from two angles and see it in the kind of depth perspective that neither one alone could achieve.

ONE VERY IMPORTANT DISTINCTION that is often overlooked in marital relations is the difference between the *content* and the *process* of problem resolution. The *content* is the actual issue that makes up the problem: in-laws coming to visit, how to spend money, who does the dishes and when, where to put the new sofa. The *process* refers to how a couple actually goes about resolving the problem: do they get angry or keep calm? do they both talk at the same time? is one agressive and the other passive? are they respectful or scornful of the other's point of view? do they mix irrelevant issues into the conversation?

The *process* of marital interaction is by far the more crucial element. No matter how complex the content of a problem may be, a couple will be able to resolve it if they have developed an effective and harmonious process of communication. When the process level of the relationship is characterized by love, respect, and consideration, the resolution of even the most difficult problems is only a matter of time.

THE MARRIAGE IDEAL

The most powerful factor for ensuring a happy marriage is the sharing of strong spiritual dedication. In a spiritual marriage each partner knows that if it comes to a choice between being petty, hurt, and spiteful, or being broad-minded, strong, and forgiving, their mate will strive to live the higher way.

Marriage partners can develop a deep level of trust when each knows that the other is thus dedicated to doing God's Will. When the loyalties of both husband and wife are sincerely directed toward the living of truth, beauty, and goodness within their relationship, marriage can begin to approach its ideal state.

In the spiritually unified marriage, God is the third person in the relationship. The union is a triangular bond with God at the top. The man and woman each know that the other's primary loyalty is to the Father and to the doing of His Will. Each partner has his own strong relationship with God which has priority even over the marital relationship.

When each partner knows that the other has such primary loyalties, the couple has an immensely powerful tool for resolving difficulties that arise between them. If they each go apart to pray, asking for the Father's inner guidance in dealing with a problem, and they try to act according to His Will, the resultant transformations in attitude and approach will dissolve any tensions between them. Such spiritual practices radically improve their *process* of communication, rendering them genuinely loving and supportive of each other.

ANOTHER CRUCIAL FACTOR in ideal marital fulfillment is that the couple have higher goals to reach for, goals that transcend the relationship itself. Pictured symbolically, a man and woman should not only stare raptly into each other's eyes but should also be looking out ahead in the same direction toward a common horizon.

Just as it is important for an individual to be working toward something greater than himself, it is important for a couple to have some greater devotion to which they can commonly address their energies. Many couples find such fulfillment in the raising of children, a project which demands their full dedication.

Couples with strong spiritual commitments may develop themselves as teams in service to humanity. They combine their individual partnerships with God into a marital partnership dedicated to His work. Each partner encourages and contributes to the spiritual service efforts of the other, resulting in greater accomplishments than either could have achieved in isolation.

When a man and a woman work toward the same transcendent goals, the bonds of their love and respect for each other are mightily strengthened and the world benefits from their united efforts.

THE SPIRITUAL LIFE OF THE FAMILY

Each of the several individuals within a family unit has his or her own needs. And each person's needs bump up against the needs of the others. Numerous personal conflicts arise during the course of a typical family day. Spiritual inspiration can become the master harmonizer in family life. It is largely the parents' value structure that determines how family conflicts are resolved.

If we as parents develop the habit of seeking spiritual guidance in establishing value guidelines, and if we encourage our children to develop a living connection with God, our families will be able to evolve standards of interaction that are satisfying and effective. If little Cindy sees that her parents talk with God and that they try to be loving and generous, eventually that has an impact on how she treats her brothers and sisters and everyone else around her.

The Father's love and wisdom *can* begin to pattern our family relationships. Our natural selfish tendencies then begin to recede as the spiritual urge to give unselfishly grows.

BECAUSE OF ITS INTENSE INTIMACY, family living makes great demands on us. As parents we can respond in two ways to such pressures: we can buckle under the strain and retreat to selfish and unloving interactions, or we can rise to the challenge, struggling to adapt our inner spiritual convictions to the daily demands of family life.

Just as diamonds form from coal under intense and continuous pressure, some of the most lustrous of human qualities develop in spiritual response to the stresses of family life. Family pressures can lead us either to personality deterioration or to personality growth. The results depend entirely on how we choose to respond to the inherent challenges.

EACH FAMILY HAS THE opportunity to evolve its own unique spiritual culture. The most powerful influence on growing children is the surrounding environment of the home. By suffusing our families' daily routines with spiritual references and activities we can provide a powerful atmosphere of spiritual reality for our children.

If God becomes a pervasive member of the household, children early develop their own relationships with Him. When we as parents naturally refer to the Father in heaven and often spend time communing with Him, our children are effectively introduced to the personal sharing that they too can have with God. It is important that we not pressure our children to believe what we believe. But if prayer, worship, and spiritual discussion are a regular part of our home culture, our children will naturally explore and develop their own spiritual lives.

THE FAMILY IS THE birthplace of love. Most of us first experience loving and being loved within a family. The quality and consistency of love in our early family lives can have a profound effect on our later growth.

It is most important that, as parents, we sincerely and consistently love our children. Regardless of variations in parenting philosophy, our children know whether we love them or not, and that is the most crucial factor in their healthy development. Their ability to respect themselves, to love others and to accept the love of others for them is affected by the quality of love we provide for them early in life.

While we must discipline and guide our children, we should avoid using our love as leverage to make them behave appropriately. Too many parents become angry or distant when their children do something wrong. They maintain a cold, unloving attitude as a sort of punishment. There should be clear consequences for misbehavior, but withdrawal of love should not be one of them.

Instead, we can structure the rules of the home so that there are clear and consistent rewards and punishments to teach our children appropriate behavior. When they do right, they are rewarded; when they do wrong, they are punished according to the well established rules of the home. But they should know at all times that we love them regardless of how they behave. With practice we can learn to be consistently loving and supportive while at the same time remaining firm in our application of the household rules.

IN THE SPIRITUALLY HEALTHY family, wise love is the primary ingredient, and as parents, all parts of our personalities become mobilized by such overriding affection. We devote large amounts of material energy to the physical maintenance of the home life. Our minds seek and coordinate information on wise man-woman relations and effective child-rearing practices. We evolve a strong working partnership with the inner Spirit, constantly trying to bring the Father's Will into the structure of our home lives. And our souls are much enriched by the accumulation of many experiences of applied loving. In positive response to the demands of family life, our entire personalities move ahead at full throttle.

AS ALLUDED TO BRIEFLY at the beginning of the chapter, the quality of family life has a major impact on the vigor of a civilization. A society is healthy to the extent that spiritual values predominate in the home.

If our families are unloving, materially oriented, and motivated primarily by self-gratification, then our society will be shortsighted, lazy, and uninspired. If, however, we stabilize our family lives with spiritual ideals, if we create a stimulating and affectionate environment for our children, and if we encourage them to develop their own strong inner relationships with God, then our society will flourish as a result of the efforts of a productive and fulfilled citizenry.

FAMILY LIFE AND GOD-CONCEPTS

Our concepts of God form as a result of two types of experience: the outer experience of daily events and relationships, and the inner experience of directly relating to God. In the first category of outer experience, it is our early family lives that have the most profound effect on the formation of our God-concepts. Early in life we are largely dependent on our parents for our impressions of God.

From the time of birth we are involved in a non-stop process of reaching conclusions about reality. As children, our reality is mainly controlled by our parents. Depending on the environment our parents provide, we can conclude that existence is fearful, undependable, and hostile, or we can conclude that it is supportive, consistent, and loving. We carry conclusions like these with us into later adult life.

As we mature, we form attitudes toward our parents as the authors of the reality which surrounds us. They establish the structure of the home environment; they are the central personalities in our lives.

At a certain point we begin to realize that there are parts of reality that our parents do not control. From that time on we increasingly establish our independence from our parents and go in search of other authorities from whom we can learn about reality. If we continue our search we eventually come around to realizing that God is the true parent of our personalities and the author and controller of all reality.

Because of the parallel between the role of parents in our early lives and God's role in our later adult lives, we bring many of our early conclusions about our parents to our budding relationships with God. If our parents were unloving and hostile, we tend to carry a legacy of fear and resentment into our relationship with the Father. We see God as forbidding and heartless, a punishing, judgemental deity.

Fortunately, because our concepts of God are strongly influenced by direct experience with the inner Spirit, as soon as we begin relating directly to the Father, our God-concepts begin to change. At first it is difficult for us to overcome negative parent-based God-concepts; we do not trust God. But slowly the inner experience of God's love and support begins to melt our suspicions, and we open ourselves to receive a new understanding of what God is *really* like.

If we were fortunate enough to have been raised by spiritually loving parents, we approach God with trust. We have learned that reality is good and that higher authorities have our best interests at heart. It is natural for us to transfer these early childhood conclusions to our blossoming relationship with God. And as our personal experience of the Father begins to grow, our early conclusions are fully confirmed.

AS PARENTS WE CAN experience further expansion of our God-concepts. Through loving our own children and going through the trials and tribulations of their growth, we gain valuable insights into how profoundly and patiently the Father loves us, His spiritual children. We have the opportunity to emulate the Father's nature within the living laboratory of our families. By trying to channel the Father's love to our children we slowly become more like God in our own ability to love.

IN CONCLUSION, FAMILY LIFE is incomparably valuable because it manages within one human institution to include so many different critical functions. It preserves and uplifts civilization. It encourages the spiritual development of both parents and children. It introduces children to the parental nature of the God-man relationship. It joins man and woman in life-long cooperative partnership. And it provides a context in which the most intimate human bonds can grow.

Living in a human family is the precursor to living as a spiritual child in the Father's universal family. Whether considered on the human level or on the celestial level, family is the seed-bed in which love can germinate man's deepest relationships.

PART III

Viewpoints:
The Personality's Perspective

Introduction to Part III

EVERY NOW AND AGAIN while hiking along a scenic mountain path, the trees thin out along the edge of a cliff and we come to a viewpoint, a special spot where we can look out over a large expanse of the surrounding country. Here we gain a sense of the distance we have traveled and the distance we have yet to travel. Such a viewpoint is a rest-stop where we can pause to appreciate our present place within the larger journey.

When we overlook the countryside from such a viewpoint, our appreciation of the unique spot on which we are standing deepens in response to the vastness which surrounds us. We sense ourselves in relation to larger things and are filled with awe. And when we resume our journey it is with a new and profound appreciation of how privileged we are to be walking a path through such grandeur.

Every now and again while progressing along the path of life, we reach a clear and open spot way up in the high country of spiritual realization—a "viewpoint" from which we can look out over the vast expanse of life, the past lands already traveled, and the unexplored territories ahead.

From this pinnacle we can survey the horizons of our existence. We are awed at the richness and beauty of the reality spread out before us. We can see the exciting destinations that await us in the distance, and we rejoice in the splendor of the experiential mountains and valleys through which we have already passed.

OUR VIEWPOINT ON EXISTENCE has a major impact on how we live. The reflective thinker asks himself, "What is reality? What is my purpose and place within it?" How we answer such questions can make the difference between an existence of hopeless apathy and a joyously fulfilled and dynamic life.

Our outlook is tremendously broadened when we look at life from the heights of a spiritual viewpoint. Life events come into clear perspective in relation to the vastness of our spiritual surroundings. Priorities line up in order. As we walk life's path, we are refreshed and strengthened by the view along the high road of spiritual striving.

CHAPTER

8

Looking at Life
and Afterlife

EACH PERSON FORMS A VIEWPOINT ON LIFE

Whether we consciously realize it or not, we are constantly reaching conclusions about existence. We develop opinions about reality which combine to form our overall viewpoint on life. We may decide that existence is exciting, challenging, supportive, and generally speaking, a wonderful place in which to be. Alternatively, we may conclude that life is brutal, painful, hopeless, ugly; that it is a vale of tears, a jungle struggle in which the meager prize of survival goes to those who are the most ruthless.

When influential individuals within a society espouse a certain viewpoint, large numbers of people may superficially adopt it as a philosophy of living. Such popular philosophies may begin to pattern the viewpoint of an entire civilization.

The vigor of both individuals and civilizations depends on their outlook on life. And no factor more greatly influences the quality of our viewpoint than the depth of our spiritual faith.

THE VIEWPOINT OF FAITH

Because of our very natures, we find ourselves in a frustrating dilemma. We are finite physical beings filled with self-centered urges, struggling for existence in a demanding and far less than perfect world. And yet, while we are so obviously finite and limited, we have within us a spiritual spark of infinity, a celestial Presence which impels us to reach for the highest spiritual ideals.

There is a huge gap between these two poles in our personalities. If we live spiritually, we engage in a continuing effort to bridge that gap, to integrate these divergent urges within our personalities. The bridging of that gap requires a leap of faith.

Faith sustains us as we attempt to close the gap between our spiritual and material natures. The viewpoint of faith gives rise to unshakeable confidence that our spiritual struggles will result in increasing success and eventual self-mastery.

WHILE WE EACH form our own unique viewpoint, there are several major questions that most of us try to answer.

- Is there a God?
- Is the universe coordinated?
- Are there absolute values?
- Is there a purpose to life?
- Is life eternal?
- Is each person ultimately alone?

These key questions are considered in the following sections along with the conclusions to them which grow out of a faith viewpoint on life.

IS THERE A GOD?

This is the fundamental question. Is there a higher and perfect Presence who is the Creator of reality or did reality just "happen"? Is there an infinite Being to whom we can relate or are we our own highest authority?

THE EXISTENCE OF GOD is the very foundation on which the viewpoint of faith is built. All other facets of the faith outlook are set within this foundation. *There is a God!* He is the Source of all reality, the Center around which all things revolve. He sustains existence. Without Him there would be nothing. He is perfect in *every* way.

To science, God is the first Cause of physical reality and the maintainer of all physical laws and relationships. From an intellectual standpoint, God is the source of all mind, the generous bestower of awareness. Spiritually, God is the origin of the highest values of truth, beauty, and goodness. And in direct relationship to man, God is an infinitely loving and personal spiritual Father.

IS THE UNIVERSE COORDINATED?

Is reality simply a huge game of chance? Is existence simply a series of blindly colliding factors or is it purposeful and organized? Either there is an overall plan to reality or the universe is the result of a series of random accidents.

FROM A FAITH VIEWPOINT, all of reality is unfolding according to a vast and purposeful plan. God knows what is going on; His reality is ordered. On the largest scale God's Will patterns the universe; even the galaxies spin by His design.

Each thing and person within His Creation has an important part to play in the evolving universe panorama. While the over-control of reality as a whole rests with God, He has given us free-will control over those small parts of reality which are our personalities. We can thus choose to align our lives with God's evolving plan or we can depart from it and strike out on our own isolated tangent away from reality.

FROM OUR LIMITED FINITE position it is sometimes difficult to discern the overall order and coordination of reality. At times life may seem unreasonable and confusing. But if we look at life from a faith viewpoint, we recognize that the overall direction of life is toward higher goals and greater coordination, despite temporary set-backs. We know internally that this is true even when it might appear otherwise from our limited human perspective.

Despite the complexities and challenges of life, we do not fear being lost in the cosmic shuffle. We have faith that God's reality makes sense and that we have a special place within it. We positively know that if we strive for spiritual growth we will succeed, for the Father has provided an ordered existence within which we can progress.

ARE THERE ABSOLUTE VALUES?

Some thinkers claim that there are clear values of right and wrong or good and evil. Others claim that because we measure good or evil within our personal experience and each of us has different experiences, there is no such thing as absolute good or evil. They say it is all relative; it all depends on a person's belief system. Knocking an old man over the head to steal his money is fine if your personal values support such an action. What is evil for one person may be good for another. There is no objective right or wrong.

A FAITH STANCE IMPLIES that indeed there are absolute values. God is the source of all that is right and good. If we were all alone in forming our values and there was no God, then values would indeed be only relative. But in seeking and finding God we locate an absolute value guide. The Father is the epitome of what is true, good, and beautiful in reality. Just as a compass needle is drawn inevitably north toward the earth's magnetic pole, so the spiritual seeker is drawn unerringly Godward in his quest for higher values.

Because God is the source of all true values, the more God-seeking two individuals become the more harmonious will be their two value systems. If we all would sincerely consult God for what is right, the absolute value of love would quickly rule the world.

VALUES ARE THE very medium of decision making, the raw material of spiritual living. Every situation is filled with value content. When we reach for God within a situation, we reach for true values; we reach for reality itself.

IS THERE A PURPOSE TO LIFE?

Either life has no underlying purpose and we are just passing time eating, sleeping, working for self-maintenance, and procreating, or we are here for a higher purpose, a reason that transcends our mere functional daily activities. Either there is an overarching goal to life and we can choose to head toward it, or life is meaningless and we are simply running in place.

FAITH ASSERTS THAT THERE is a clear purpose in life: to know God increasingly and become more like Him. There is a thrilling destination towards which we can move. We can strive to reach for the perfection of the Father.

The process of living is not aimless; it is most definitely directional. Each day presents us with a challenging new stretch of road to travel in our journey Godward. Reality is chock-full of meaning and purpose. The goals of the spiritual life are worthy of our total effort. Existence is an exhilarating, ever more stimulating voyage upward and inward to the goal of God.

The primary goals of living are spiritual. Material reality is merely the backdrop, the passing scenery for the unfolding of a spiritual drama. Loving God and doing His Will is what life is all about. The passing activities of daily life are means to the end of spiritual transformation.

When we attempt to uplift our common activities with spiritual inspiration, we enter into an entirely different way of living. The most fleeting interaction with another person becomes an opportunity for sharing the Father's love, for transforming ourselves and elevating the surrounding reality of daily life. The higher values that are there all the time become apparent. We realize that a spiritual purpose underlies *all* of reality.

APATHY AND DEJECTION RESULT from a worldview that is meaningless, directionless. Why go on, when there is nowhere to go? If there is no higher purpose to life, why live? Without transcendent goals, life becomes monotonous. Short term purposes, limited gratification, mundane fulfillments are not enough to make life worthwhile. There is nothing *profoundly* exciting in a materialistic view of reality, nothing to kindle the imagination and stimulate us to loftier efforts.

The discovery of the goal of perfection in relationship with God has a powerful impact on us. Here is a goal worth every ounce of effort we can expend. Here is a purpose to pursue which can never grow dull or boring. The spiritually purposeful personality thrives on life; it hums along happily in high gear.

In the God-seeking adventure, we know that we have found an inexhaustible and totally satisfying purpose for living. What could be more motivating? Unlimited growth is the invigorating promise. The spiritual transformation of everyday reality is the ongoing reward.

Amidst the turbulent events and transient desires of our human lives, spiritual goals stand out as high and clear as a stable lighthouse beam in the midst of an ocean storm. The dependable beacon of a transcendent spiritual objective steadies and orients us.

The goal of perfection is an all-encompassing standard according to which the lesser goals of temporal existence can be aligned. Every life activity gains meaning when measured by such a standard. When we try to live in accordance with this highest of purposes, our personalities grow increasingly stable and unified.

IF OUR GOALS reach only as far as the borders of our own personalities, we can never grow beyond our own present limitations. Only by reaching for a purpose that is higher than ourselves can we ever hope to become greater than we presently are. And only by reaching for the Father's perfection itself, can we assure ourselves a future of self-expanding growth that never ends.

IS LIFE ETERNAL?

One way of looking at life is that we have sixty or seventy years worth of experience available to us, and when the old body shuts down that is the end. No more conscious awareness, no more relationships, no more growth, nothing!

Since time immemorial, however, people have entertained an alternate view: that this life is simply the entryway to a greater and never-ending existence; that what is begun in the human life is destined for completion beyond the doorway of death. Belief in an afterlife has striking implications for how we live in the here and now.

FROM THE VIEWPOINT OF FAITH, eternal life is logical. It makes no sense that God would create us with free will, place us within an environment that stimulates decisions and growth, provide us with a perfect fragment of Himself as a loving guide, and then cut off our existence just when we were beginning to reach for our potentials.

Returning to an earlier analogy, human existence without afterlife would make about as much sense as an airplane that is meant to fly, picking up speed for take-off only to smash into a brick wall at the end of the runway. Why construct planes to fly if they are destined for destruction before ever lifting off the ground? Why would God equip us with the potential for unlimited spiritual growth only to destroy us at the very entrance to the higher existence for which we were created?

Death is the doorway that opens into the next and higher stage of existence. Everything of worth for which we strive in this life is destined for continuation and eventual completion in the next. Life is not a dead-end; it is not futile.

To the sincere child of faith, death holds no threat. From a faith viewpoint, we can look ahead to the afterlife with real anticipation, knowing that the Father has lovingly prepared a stimulating and satisfying existence of eternal progress for us. We totally trust God to do what is best for us.

IN HIS INFINITE WISDOM the Father has provided an earthly existence that challenges us to struggle for what is right, and thus grow. Such growth resulting from our sincere efforts characterizes the afterlife as well. Mere physical death does not transfer us to a realm of blissful perfection where we do nothing but recline on clouds and play harps all day long. We continue to earn our growth by decisions and actions.

The approach to perfection is made along the road of actual experience. Each time we act in harmony with the Father's Will, each time we follow the leading of His inner Spirit, we take one more experiential step toward perfection.

And it is right that we must thus earn perfection in the afterlife. We can only lay claim to that progress which we have experientially gained. To be made perfect suddenly by a celestial snap of the fingers would be contrary to the whole purpose of eternal life. The reason that we reach for perfection is not simply to *be* perfect, but to go through the experience of *becoming* perfect. God could make us perfect any time He wanted to. But then He would be depriving us of the incredible rewards of reaching perfection through our own efforts.

Picture a man climbing along a lush forest path which eventually leads to the top of a ridge of hills. His goal is to get to the ridge. But if he were suddenly transported there he would never experience the many scenes of beauty along the path. And he would not have the opportunity to develop his strength while actually climbing to the top. The end goal of being at the top of the ridge would be empty and meaningless without the actual process of climbing there.

The experiences gained along the way are part of what makes any destination worth achieving. So it is with the ascent toward perfection in the afterlife. It is the actual process of growing spiritually, of earning and thus possessing each step along the way, that makes the ultimate prize of perfection worth striving for.

THE WAY THAT WE live is profoundly affected by faith in eternal life. The realization that eternity begins right here and now and that life will not be cut short within a few years makes a very real difference in how we spend our time during the human life.

For one thing, given an eternity perspective, it does not make much sense to avoid dealing with difficult situations. From a time-bound viewpoint, if we can put off resolving an unpleasant situation for long enough, we can just leave it behind when we die. But if our outlook includes eternal life, what we avoid in this life we know we will eventually have to resolve in the afterlife.

If we are reaching for perfection, there is no use postponing difficult growth since somewhere along the way we will have to deal with it anyway. And the sooner we resolve a problem that we know exists, the sooner we can move on to greater and more rewarding challenges.

If we are running a race, trying to avoid crossing the starting line doesn't make much sense. If we assume that life is eternal and our goal is growth toward perfection, procrastination in this life doesn't make much sense either.

FROM A TIME-BOUND viewpoint, all our efforts to become more loving and God-like are destined to be cut short by death. So why try in the first place? We might as well give up on progress. Trying to grow does not make sense when it all ends in nothing but personal destruction.

From a faith viewpoint, however, we continue our efforts in the afterlife. We take our human accomplishments with us through the portals of death. The partial progress we have made during the human life will not be cut off in the middle; we shall have the opportunity to make our most noble ambitions real in the afterlife.

Working in this life to become a better person, struggling to build a more noble character, makes sense. Spiritual goals can indeed be reached. What we begin in time we are destined to complete in eternity.

WHEN WE SEE LIFE from the eternity outlook, we develop a deep sense of patience. There is no point in feeling pressured and rushed about life if there is no looming deadline before which we must get everything done. Why be impatient with ourselves when the Father is so superbly patient with us that He has given us an unlimited amount of time in which to grow? Since perfection is an absolute goal, we deserve an eternal time period in which to reach it.

The idealistic person often becomes frustrated because there is so much to do, there are so many goals to reach for, and he feels so inadequate to the task. The eternity viewpoint provides solace for such a frustrated idealist; all his ideals will be realized in the fullness of the afterlife.

Once he recognizes this truth he can patiently address those goals which have the highest present priority, knowing that what he sets aside is not lost but simply relegated to a later time. He realizes he cannot do all things at once. But his faith assures him that he will indeed enjoy the opportunity to do *all* worthwhile things in the fullness of eternal life.

From an eternity viewpoint, it is more important that we do things in a right and full way than that we simply get them done and over with. *What* we accomplish in life is less important than *how* we accomplish it. If we reach just one higher life goal with spiritual integrity, we are much farther ahead than if we accomplish a hundred lesser goals in a shallow and deceptive manner. The quality of our accomplishments is primary; the quantity is secondary.

HAVING FAITH IN ETERNAL life leads us to a thorough attitude of enthusiasm about existence. Our lives are filled with anticipation of the exciting future that lies ahead, and this excitement reflects back into the lives that we are presently leading.

It is exhilarating to think that eternity starts now. And it is to be filled with spiritual adventures that are so grand that we cannot even begin to imagine them. Never will reality become routine; boredom cannot exist in a universe that constantly challenges us to new growth. The universe is in fact a vast "universe-ity", an unlimited school of experiential growth, an ever-lasting learning center for our expanding souls.

The eternity outlook results in an unparalleled sense of inner peace. The threat of termination no longer hangs over life. Having faith, we know that in a spiritual sense, nothing can harm us; regardless of material calamity, our souls will survive. We enjoy an unshakeable sense of assurance and inner calm.

We know that if we stand courageously by our highest principles we will ultimately triumph, if not in this life then in the next. Our profound confidence in the Father's plan of eternal life gives rise to an astonishing type of inner tranquility that is impervious to the upheavals of human life. Fear has no place in a universe of eternal progress.

THERE IS ONLY ONE thing which we should justifiably fear: separation from God. To leave God behind is to depart from reality and ultimately leads to personality suicide. Personality death does in fact exist. But God does not destroy us. We have the responsibility for our own survival or non-survival.

The afterlife is an existence of progressive growth Godward, of working to become more true, good, and beautiful in cooperation with the spiritual Guide within. It is a life of robust courage and active spiritual achievement. It is not simply continuing existence; it requires that we humbly love God and sincerely dedicate ourselves to doing His Will.

We have the choice of either accepting or rejecting such an afterlife existence. If we do not wish to participate, we are not forced to.

For the person who rejects the pursuits of the spiritual life, physical death ends up being total personality death as well. He simply ceases to exist. He doesn't want to put forth the effort to struggle with his imperfections and grow. He, in effect, chooses not to exist rather than take up the demanding goals of the afterlife. As is always the case, God respects man's free will choice.

THE CLOSING POINT in our consideration of eternal life focuses on the afterlife as being *personal.* Survival after death is not similar to a drop of water merging with the ocean. The individuality of our personalities is not lost in the afterlife. The Father created each of us as a distinct personality for a purpose. Each of us, as we grow closer to God, actualizes spiritual qualities that are special, that only we can bring to fruition. We each offer a contribution to reality that is ours alone, that springs from the unique personality that the Father has given us.

In the afterlife we are capable of having satisfying personal relationships with God and with other surviving personalities. We can each continue to plumb the potentials of our own unique temperament. Free will personality is the Father's greatest gift to man; He does not demand it back at physical death.

IS EACH PERSON ULTIMATELY ALONE?

Some people conclude that each of us is, in an ultimate sense, isolated in reality. Such a viewpoint assumes, "No one else can feel what I feel. I can never share the deepest parts of myself with another person. I am alone, an unimportant individual drifting through life. Inner loneliness is my fate, and I must learn to live with it."

IF WE HAVE A FAITH viewpoint, however, we work with very different assumptions. From a faith perspective, each of us is intimately connected with other people, and we can share deeply with them. The two dependable truths that ensure such connection are that God is our loving Father, and that His Spirit presence lives right within us.

A faith viewpoint boldly asserts, "I am a child of God and I am enveloped by His love. His Spirit resides deep within me and intimately shares all of my feelings and experiences. He knows all my yearnings, joys, triumphs, conflicts, and struggles. I do not go through life alone; God is my inner friend and traveling companion. He has given a part of Himself to be with me at all times.

And because He has given a similar fragment of Himself to every other person, I have an inner bond in common with my fellows. We are *all* His children and share His loving overcare. I am not alone and adrift. I am connected by love to every other person in the Father's universal family."

FAITH VERSUS FEAR

Each person's attitude toward life falls somewhere along a continuum which has total fear at one end and total faith at the other. The large majority of us fall somewhere in between. Sometimes we're dominated by fear and sometimes we open ourselves to faith. Spiritual growth involves a movement away from a fearful outlook and toward a faithful outlook.

We cannot look into the future; we cannot know what tomorrow will bring. Given such lack of foreknowledge, we naturally experience some uncertainty about life. We are, in some respects, like a blind man inching down a long hallway with hands outstretched, trying to sense what lies out ahead. If he thinks wild beasts are lurking in the hallway, he will retreat in fear. If, however, he believes that the hallway is filled with old friends, he will move forward joyfully to greet them.

The situation is similar for us as we move into the unknown future. Depending on what we think awaits us, what we think life is like, we will either approach with eagerness or retreat in fear.

If we have a fearful outlook on life, our assumptions are that existence is dangerous and that we must protect ourselves against it. We must barricade ourselves against reality in order not to be run over and destroyed by it. Rather than venturing out into life, we pull into the safe hole of a very limited existence. We try to shut out new relationships and events because they threaten us. We hide as best we can from a universe which we feel is hostile and frightening.

When our outlook is one of faith, we live an utterly different kind of life. We still encounter the vacuum of the unknown future; that is a given in human life. But we assume that the Father has created a reality that works to our ultimate benefit. We feel trusting and optimistic toward the unknown future. Our reality assumptions are that life is good, that the universe is a friendly and supportive place.

We certainly experience hardship and struggle in dealing with life's problems, but our assumption is that as we resolve such problems they result in our eventual growth. Given such faith assumptions, we march out boldly into life, unafraid of its rigors, confident that through the wilful pursuit of spiritual ideals we will overcome all obstacles.

This distinction between a faith or fear attitude has tremendous implications for our growth and progress at any particular choice-point. For instance, suppose we've recently made a new friend and are having a hard time communicating clearly with him. When faced with such a difficult situation, we can move in one of two directions. If we are afraid that we will be hurt, we retreat from the relationship and fail to grow.

If, however, we have developed a faith outlook on life, we have come to expect that when we put out a sincere effort we often succeed; so we approach the relationship anew, resolve the difficulty, and grow stronger.

Fear and faith are both powerful moving forces within us. Fear moves us to retreat away from life; it destroys hope and leads to despair. Faith moves us toward the Father and higher reality. It fosters courage and strength of character and leads to exuberant living.

Once again, as at all crucial crossroads in life, human will has full responsibility for choosing between the low road of fear which ends in oblivion, and the high road of faith which spirals ever up toward the infinite loving Father of all creation.

WITHOUT THE FOUNDATION of personal spiritual faith, we cannot have true happiness. And when we have faith no outward circumstance can destroy our sense of "rightness" about life. The unshakeable joy of the faith viewpoint is the treasure for which people have searched throughout human history. We can have it if we will reach out to God with sincere desire and childlike trust.

THE DIFFERENCE BETWEEN FAITH AND BELIEF

There is a distinct difference between faith and belief. If we believe something, we accept it intellectually. We acknowledge that it is a valid idea. Beliefs occur in our minds; they are merely a species of thought.

Faith, however, involves our entire personalities. Faith is an actual way of living. It demands that we transform our lives in accordance with what we have faith in.

If we *believe* in God, we simply acknowledge that He exists without necessarily doing anything about it. If we have *faith* in God, we live in vital interaction with Him. We actually change ourselves in response to our growing understanding of the Father's Will. Belief merely implies that we recognize God. Faith requires that we become God-like.

LIVING RELIGION NEVER drops to the dead level of mere intellectual belief. Intellectual belief alone is only the ghost of animated religion. Belief is simply a passive acceptance of established doctrines, sedimented and inert.

Real religion, on the other hand, is thrillingly alive, ever changing and growing in response to the challenge of the Father's inner Spirit. Dynamic faith is and continues to be an actual way of living with God.

WHY DOES GOD ALLOW EVIL AND SUFFERING?

One of the most often-asked religious questions concerns the obvious evil and suffering that exist in the world. If God is good and all-powerful why does He allow such negative realities to occur? Why do young children fall ill and die? Why are innocent people destroyed in the horror of war? The faith of many an individual has been shaken by the deeply personal doubts that arise when tragedy strikes or when evil runs rampant.

In attempting to resolve this dilemma it is important to keep three primary truths in mind:

1. God has given man free-will control over himself and his environment.

2. Death is not a tragic dead end, but rather a passageway to a higher life.

3. From a larger spiritual perspective, good inevitably triumphs over evil.

1. IF WE ARE TO HAVE true free will then we must be as free to choose evil as to choose good. If God were to allow us to do good but blocked our free will whenever we contemplated doing evil, we would not really have a choice. We would be puppets without real self-control. If when we came to a choice between being kind or being cruel, God always made us kind, we would be little more than machines. To have a choice to go in only one direction is not to have a choice at all. In order to prevent man from doing evil, God would have to deprive him of free will.

Man himself controls the extent of much of the evil and suffering that surrounds him. The reason that the world is at times an evil and ugly place is that, to a large degree, individuals within the larger civilization have not yet chosen to be led by the Spirit within them.

As time progresses, if increasing numbers of people try to live God-centered lives, all parts of civilization will flourish and our world will become a very different kind of place. We can create a transformed world only when we as individuals are transformed.

2. THE MOST TRAGIC OCCURRENCE for many people is the death of someone they love, especially someone who dies unjustly or at a young age. "How can God allow such tragedy?" they ask.

From a materialistic viewpoint, death is the final and irrevocable end of a person's existence. That indeed is tragic. But then from a faith viewpoint that is not what death is at all! The separation of death is not permanent, but temporary. When people we love die, they move on to a new stage of existence. And when we who survive them inevitably pass on in our turn, we can look forward to a joyful reunion with them.

It's as if all our family and friends moved to a country far away and eventually, after many years, we joined them there. What a superb occasion for celebration!

Seen from the faith viewpoint, death is not the ultimate human tragedy but rather the natural entryway to the afterlife. Some of us depart sooner and some later, but the relatively short separation is quite bearable when we know that our close companions have passed on to an intriguing place, and that we are due to join them there before long.

Having faith in survival, we put death in a much larger perspective. We begin to see that the Father allows physical death, premature and otherwise, because He has glorious plans for us in the afterlife.

Thus the fact that millions of people have died in the senseless destruction of war, while it may be hard for their survivors to bear, is not tragic in an ultimate sense. They are not necessarily gone forever. Death does not have to cut off their growth in mid-stream. They can choose to continue on in the afterlife.

In trying to understand why God allows evil and suffering, we have noted that evil is a byproduct of our having free will. And it continues to exist only to the extent that we fail to follow the Father's Will. We have also noted that the scale of human tragedy shrinks considerably when we see death as the entrance to an eternal afterlife of perfecting growth.

3. THE LAST POINT to consider is that in the Father's universe evil is only a temporary and unreal phenomenon. In the long run good will triumph and evil will fade increasingly into nonreality. It may appear at times that evil conquers good. But that is an illusion born of our time-bound frame of reference. Evil is a shadow of reality that cannot sustain itself. Goodness, rooted in God, is real and endures forever.

The evils of this world are a transient part of reality. The wars, the famine, the barbaric cruelty that occasionally sweep across entire nations are but the passing storms of mankind's adolescence. Such evil may temporarily loom large as a result of the acts of short-sighted men and women.

But in the fullness of time the shadow of evil will give way to the illumination of good. When the light comes the shadow departs. As we progressively embrace God's goodness, the temporary evils of our transitional age will retreat into the back alleys of unreality.

GOD HAS GIVEN US responsibility for our world. Civilization is in the midst of a millenia-long struggle of growth toward a higher destiny. There will come a time when man has developed real control over himself and his environment, when human relations are dominated by love and peace, and a responsible science has secured a world of plenty and long life for all peoples. In such a world of the future, evil and suffering will have faded far into the background of human existence.

But man can only approach his utopian potential in a hard-earned, step-by-step process of slow civilizational evolution. He has a long way to go. And so long as he refuses wholeheartedly to embrace spiritual priorities he will reap the harvest of hate and cruelty that results from a materialistic viewpoint. The degree of suffering in the world is largely determined by man himself. God's Will is for a much better world. But the world will change only as mankind freely seeks and implements His Will.

CIVILIZATION'S VIEWPOINT: PAST, PRESENT, AND FUTURE

As previously mentioned, not only individuals but entire civilizations evolve a viewpoint, a way of looking at reality. The worldview of a civilization is constantly changing to meet the advancing needs of its people. Our present civilization is on the verge of a tremendous shift in its worldview.

Through much of the last two thousand years man's worldview was dominated by strong institutional religious influences. The religious clergy largely determined peoples' behavior and outlook, dictating standards on everything from moral codes to the nature of the physical universe. For many centuries their authority had been complete and unchallenged.

In the sixteenth century, science began increasingly to influence the worldview of the western world. It offered explanations of physical reality, and on many fronts successfully challenged the authority of the religious institutions. It loosened the grip of the clergy on the minds of the general populace. Science encouraged the start of a technological wave of progress that has moved powerfully forward, revolutionizing world civilization over the past five hundred years.

Scientific progress is highly desirable and should continue. But it has spawned a viewpoint that has resulted in great spiritual confusion. While science justifiably attempted to undermine the dictatorship of sixteenth century organized religion, it made a great mistake in attacking the reality of God. The unfortunate view has become widespread that man is the highest authority in existence, and that with science alone he can eventually solve all problems and create a perfect world.

Despite vast technological advances this has not occurred. After two world-wide wars and under the threat of total nuclear annihilation, we are reevaluating. We are realizing that regardless of how powerful our science becomes it remains only a tool. While it enables us to do things more effectively, it cannot tell us whether what we are doing is right or wrong. Science gives us facts; for values we must look to spiritual sources.

Today's civilization is awakening to the realization that science is limited by our vision of how to use it. Science is merely a means to an end, not an end in itself. Technological progress alone will never result in an individual who can fully give and receive love and who experiences fulfillment and purpose in life. Science cannot provide a sense of intimate relationship with the Source of all reality. Such rewards are found only as a result of inner spiritual search.

OUR CIVILIZATION HAS COME to an unprecedented turning point. We are in desperate need of a spiritual and moral worldview that matches the level of our technical and intellectual sophistication. We are standing on the brink of a tremendous world-wide spiritual reawakening.

In the civilization of the future, the urge to develop a spiritually mature personality will surpass the drive for material and intellectual achievements. Our society is on the verge of discovering that human life is most satisfying when we coordinate scientific facts and intellectual ideas according to the guiding spiritual principles discovered within a living relationship with God.

It is as true for entire civilizations as for single individuals: the highest purpose for which man exists is the finding of God.

ᴐᴥᴐᴥᴐ

CHAPTER

9

How We See Ourselves

THREE TYPES OF SELF-CONCEPT

Every person forms feelings about himself. Our viewpoints on life involve more than simply our conclusions about reality on the outside. We also form conclusions about what we are like on the inside and whether or not we are pleased with ourselves. Such self-conclusions form a crucial part of our attitude toward life.

One of psychology's best documented findings is that how we see ourselves, our *self-concept,* plays a large part in how satisfied we are. If we like and respect ourselves, we are generally much happier than if we are highly self-critical. A positive self-concept is very important to a balanced spiritual life; it forms a part of the foundation from which spiritual growth springs.

There are three types of self-concept that we can have: *self-dislike, self-pride,* and *self-respect.* While each of us has some elements of all three types, usually one set of self-feelings dominates. With time and effort, we can successfully change and upgrade our self-concept.

The person who feels *self-dislike* assumes, "I am inadequate and weak, unable to deal with life. I'm not as good as other people. I am so much less than what I should be, and I have little hope of improving. I don't like myself, and I can see why other people wouldn't like me either. If there is a God, He certainly doesn't want anything to do with me."

Feeling *self-respect* leads a person to conclude, "While there is still much left to accomplish, all in all, I am pleased with myself. I am strong enough to overcome life's problems, and I'm a pretty good person. I have ideals which I have not yet attained, but with time I will achieve them. I respect my own abilities and qualities and feel that most other people like and respect me as well. I feel that God loves me as I am and wants to help me grow to reach my full potentials."

Self-pride results from such assumptions as the following: "Since I'm pretty close to perfect I don't need to improve myself. I'm much better than other people. In fact, I think I'm great. Most people are too shortsighted or too jealous to acknowledge my superiority. Well, I don't need other people! And I certainly don't need any so-called Higher Power telling me how to run my life!"

As is probably apparent by now, self-dislike and self-pride lie at the extreme ends of the self-concept spectrum. Neither one of them is satisfactory; neither one leads to fulfillment in life. Real happiness must be based on balanced self-respect. And the most powerful tools for developing self-respect are to be found in a personal relationship with God.

CHANGING SELF-DISLIKE TO SELF-RESPECT

How does a person come to dislike himself? Typically, the most influential factor in the formation of our self-concept is how other people relate to us. In forming our feelings about ourselves, we take our cues from people who are important to us, especially during our formative childhood years. Parents, siblings, close friends, and, later in life, a spouse can all have an impact on our emerging self-concept.

If such important others are unloving, critical, and abusive toward a person, if they treat him as if he is worthless, he himself will probably conclude that he is worthless. Surrounded by criticism, he will learn to be self-critical. Having no other major reference points for self-evaluation, he will take in their negative image of him and adopt it as his own. If they kick him around, he will feel he must deserve to be kicked around; so he kicks himself around as well.

Sometimes such self-dislike continues long after a person has severed his relations with those who have abused him in the past. I have seen people in therapy who are quite successful materially, but feel terrible about themselves. Such people may not remember much of the emotional pain they experienced. They may not even be able to remember where they got such negative ideas about themselves. But their damaged self-concepts remain as the grim legacy of those destructive early relationships.

The person who dislikes himself has difficulty accepting love. He is so accustomed to being unloved that he sees himself as not worthy to receive the affection of others. When others do show him affection, he often rejects it out of disbelief. He doubts their sincerity because he cannot believe that another person could actually find him lovable.

IF WE FEEL THIS way about ourselves, how can we break out of the trap of self-dislike and begin to develop a respectful self-concept? The key lies in taking our self-image cues from God rather than relying on other people for such feedback.

Other people, even if they are well-intentioned, are fallible. We cannot depend on them to accurately appraise our self-worth. The Father, however, is perfect. If we try to see ourselves in the way that He sees us, we will see ourselves as we really are. If we can begin to love ourselves in the way that the Father loves us, we will be well on our way toward developing self-respect. If we treat ourselves the way that He treats us, with compassion and caring, we cannot remain self-destructive for long.

In the process of developing self-respect, we progressively change our attitude toward ourselves. We adopt the attitude of love, tolerance, and optimism that the Father has toward us. God re-teaches us who and what we really are and how we should feel about ourselves. When we know that we are infinitely loved children of the heavenly Father, we can develop a profound form of self-respect.

Bit by bit the old faulty self-concept we took from important people in the past is replaced by the new and sublime self-concept we take from the *most* important Person. The self-feelings rooted in our human parent-child relationships give way to self-feelings arising in our relationship with the heavenly Parent.

EVEN THOUGH WE ARE far from perfect, the Father loves and respects each one of us. He is infinitely forgiving and patient with us as we climb the long ladder of spiritual growth. He knows what we go through and He supports us every step of the way.

If the perfect God of all creation feels that way about us and we are trying to emulate Him, we should feel that way about ourselves too! How absurd that we should dislike ourselves when God Himself loves us so much! We should be taking our cues from Him! We should be gentle and patient with ourselves, forgiving of our own shortcomings and respectful of our potentials. Seeing ourselves from God's viewpoint enlarges our self-respect.

If we happen to dislike ourselves, we tend to assume that everyone else, including God, dislikes us too. We conclude that we are so unlovable that even God rejects us. We project our own feelings about ourselves onto God. We assume that He sees things our way.

But that does not make sense! The Father does not take *His* lead from *us*. Instead we should take *our* lead from *Him*. He loves us perfectly regardless of how we feel about ourselves. The way *He* feels about us should uplift *our* self-concept.

When we stop imagining that God looks at things our way and realize that we should be trying to look at things His way, self-dislike fades and self-respect can begin to grow.

PUTTING FAILURE AND GUILT WHERE THEY BELONG

Failure and guilt have a real but limited role to play in spiritual growth. When we deal with them in the right way they can lead to an enhanced self-concept. Unfortunately, many people give failure and guilt much too large and important a place in their lives. If we do not put guilt and failure in proper perspective our self-concept suffers.

FAILURE CAN BE very meaningful. If we have turned the wrong way up a one-way street and suddenly see a line of cars coming our way, we know for certain we've made a mistake somewhere. From that time on we are likely to pay close attention to one-way street signs.

Every life experience, including failure, is a lesson from which we can glean valuable truth. When we feel the self-respect born of a spiritual viewpoint, we no longer find failure threatening. Instead of hiding from our mistakes, we approach them with good humor and humility. We understand why we failed and how we can succeed in similar situations in the future.

If we are wise, we have learned how to turn our failures around and transform them into springboards to future growth. Defeats in life do not trip us up; we use them as stepping stones in our Godward ascent. Failure merely spurs us on to greater efforts.

We enthusiastically explore our mistakes without flinching at the fact that we have failed. We know that the process of making mistakes and learning from them builds our personalities. The realization dawns that using failures productively is a basic method for developing a hardy character. We learn to thrive amidst even the most difficult life circumstances.

The eternity perspective helps us to be patient with ourselves when we fail. Failure is only temporary; in the fullness of eternal life we shall enjoy the opportunity to outgrow all of our inadequacies.

Failure should never cripple our attempts to grow. We should constantly be reaching for higher ideals, challenging ourselves to improve. And when, as is inevitable for a human being, we do fail, we should not lower our spiritual standards. We should not blame ourselves for failing.

Instead, we should good-naturedly acknowledge our failure and learn the lessons it has to teach us. Then stoking the fires of our loyalty to the Father's Will, we should resume our journey on life's forward path, optimistic of our ultimate success.

GUILT IS A SENTIMENT that has needlessly plagued mankind for too long. Some unfortunate people spend 90% of their day feeling guilty. In the words of one wise person, "Regret is mildew on the bread of life." Wallowing overlong in guilt sours the flavor of life and deteriorates our self-concept.

There is only one productive purpose to feelings of guilt. Sometimes we feel guilty when we have done something wrong and are trying to avoid facing up to it. In such circumstances guilt serves as a red flag that indicates that something needs to be corrected. It acts as a kind of psychological warning signal, alerting us to a trouble spot that requires our attention.

But once we realize that we are feeling guilty about something and we take action to correct what is wrong, guilt has *no more purpose!* At that point guilt is useless; in fact, if it persists it becomes downright destructive.

Unfortunately, sometimes we get stuck midway in the guilt cycle. We start to feel guilty about something and instead of finding out why and doing something about it, we try to ignore our guilt feelings. But the more we try to hide from the situation the guiltier we feel.

For instance, suppose we get impatient with a family member and pop out with an angry remark. We start feeling guilty about it. If we face our feelings, acknowledge what the guilt is about, and do something to restore love to the relationship, then our guilt will have served its purpose.

However, if we keep on trying to ignore the situation, our feelings of guilt will likely grow. When guilt mounts in this manner our self-concept begins to suffer. We lose respect for ourselves because we are not dealing with what we feel guilty about.

When handled properly, guilt can play a productive role in personality growth. It can alert us to small problems before they grow large.

Once it has served its alerting purpose, guilt should be discarded immediately. If we fail to let go of our guilt after righting the wrong which caused it in the first place, it festers within our personalities and can result in the spreading rot of self-dislike.

IN SUMMARY, WHEN WE allow failure and guilt to dominate our personalities, we can begin to feel intensely dissatisfied with ourselves. When used productively, however, they can strengthen our personalities and help us develop balanced self-respect. The key to properly using them lies in consulting the inner Spirit. With the Father's help, we can turn our failures into stepping stones to growth. And we can use guilt as a temporary red flag that alerts us to problems we need to correct.

SELF-PRIDE: A BLOCK TO SPIRITUAL GROWTH

Self-pride poses a formidable barrier to spiritual growth. This is because the prideful individual hides from his own inadequacies. He refuses to acknowledge that he has any weaknesses. Thus, he cannot begin to work on their improvement. He stays stuck in the same old negative patterns of living, all the while insisting that there is absolutely nothing wrong with him.

Self-pride leads to a type of spiritual blindness. The prideful person comes to believe that he himself is the highest source of truth. Thus he is self-blinded to anything higher than himself.

Such self-pride can only lead to a spiritual dead end. The prideful person becomes so self-satisfied that he concludes that there is no self-improvement left to attempt. Personality growth grinds to a halt.

OUR PERSONALITIES ARE always in motion; we cannot remain static. If we are not moving forward, then we are moving backward. If we are not growing stronger and happier, then bit by bit we are surely becoming weaker and less happy.

While the prideful person convinces himself that he is faultless, he is in reality slipping further and further backward into self-deception. He has stopped growing spiritually. He has isolated himself away from the challenges of reality. As reality progresses all around him and he remains stubbornly frozen in pride, he increasingly gets left behind.

Unfortunately, many prideful people, when confronted by their own obvious deterioration, react by clinging even more tenaciously to their delusions of superiority. If such pride-blindness continues its cancerous growth, it eventually leads a person to depart entirely from reality.

ON A DEEP INNER level the prideful person is frightened. He tries to hide behind his pride because he is afraid of facing his inadequacies. He is afraid that if he tries to grow he will fail.

The antidote to self-pride is a living relationship with God. When a person allows the Father into his life, he gains courage and can begin to take accurate stock of himself. He no longer has to inflate himself in his own eyes. He can acknowledge his faults because he positively knows that with God's help he can correct them.

As he gains faith, he no longer has to pretend that he's infallible. He can let down the drawbridge of his pride and walk back out into life.

When someone who hides behind self-pride realizes that there is a Person who knows all his inadequacies and loves him anyway, he can let go of the charade he has maintained. After all, he's not fooling God. With profound joy he realizes that his prideful act is unnecessary. God knows him fully and still loves him. He can drop the facade and begin living honestly as a child of the heavenly Father. He can develop *real* self-respect and begin to grow once more.

THE RESULTS OF SELF-RESPECT

Balanced self-respect is the foundation of a healthy and unified personality. When we have self-respect, we are self-assured and optimistic about ourselves. We are pleased with our present status while still reaching for the stimulating goals which remain out ahead. We like ourselves and feel worthy of others liking us.

Self-respect liberates us to love and respect our fellows. When we are assured of our own worth, we are no longer preoccupied with proving ourselves. We are free to focus on the welfare of others. Our energies can overflow to people and causes beyond ourselves. Self-respect based in a living relationship with God leads to increased service to humanity.

Self-respect releases us to be truly creative and expressive. It removes the inner block of self-doubt, allowing us to tap deep into our personality reservoirs of creative energy. When we feel good about ourselves, it becomes our delight to live productively. We rejoice in offering up the fruits of our creativity to the Father.

OUR SELF-CONCEPT AND our viewpoint on life are clearly linked. Self-respect and the viewpoint of faith go hand in hand. A faith outlook on life supports self-respect. Self-respect balances and strengthens our faith.

There is only one way that we can find the deep and lasting fulfillment of true self-respect: by developing a faith-friendship with the very Originator of respect, by becoming intimate with the majestic Father of all creation.

PART IV

Spiritual Living:
The Dynamic Personality

Introduction to Part IV

IF WE ARE FASCINATED by hummingbirds and are quick enough to capture one, there are two ways we can study it. We can hold it still and examine how it's put together. Or we can let it move around and study how it functions.

There is a similar distinction between the two different ways that scientists can study a cell under a microscope. They can take the cell apart to study its structure, how it's put together. Or they can let it move around on the slide and study its function, how it acts.

Part I of this book explored the structure of personality, the different parts and how they fit together. In this last section we will focus more on the function of personality, the personality *in action*. Part IV deals with the dynamic day-to-day process of spiritual living.

Chapter 10 takes a look at spiritual growth. How do we mature spiritually? How do inner and outer growth interact? What is the crucial role of ideals? What part do struggle and conflict play in our lives? Why is will so important to our spiritual development? How can we use problems as opportunities? Answers to all of these questions are important to a consideration of spiritual growth.

Chapter 11 explores the relationship between institutional religion and our inner spiritual lives. What important needs do institutional religions fulfill? Why all the controversy over whether religion is good or bad? What distinguishes between dead and living religion? How do our inner spiritual lives transcend our religious institutions? And what will the religion of the future look like?

Chapter 12 focuses on the day-to-day practices of our spiritual lives. How is spiritual nourishment important? What roles do prayer and worship play? How can we develop the spiritual habits needed in today's chaotic world? How do our lives change when we live spiritually? And how can we prove the existence of God?

CHAPTER

10

Spiritual Growth

THE PERFECT THERAPIST

It is human nature always to be looking for the panacea, the one solution that will remedy all problems. As society grows more complex and confusing, our search for this authoritative all-encompassing answer becomes more desperate. We join movements, pledge our loyalty to gurus, try this new therapy and that, all in an attempt to find "the answer" to our questions about how to live. Rumor has it that the editors of the magazine *Psychology Today* were so impressed with this trend that they half-seriously considered starting a regular column entitled "Panacea of the Month."

When we look for the panacea we are searching for a perfect pattern by which to guide our growth. We are seeking an authoritative source of truth, a "therapist" who can counsel us with total wisdom.

There is only one such perfect "therapist": the Father's inner Spirit. When we have problems, God's advice is always profoundly correct. He knows us with full intimacy and loves us with boundless compassion. His Spirit is always present within us whenever we need higher counsel.

God appeals to our strengths, encouraging us to reach ever higher. But He never expects of us that which we cannot yet attain. The

Father is exquisitely sensitive to where the leading edge of our growth lies.He knows just how much to challenge us so that we progress most effectively.

The final solution, the panacea, is not to be found in the outer world. The perfect Mentor waits within us.

REQUIREMENTS FOR SPIRITUAL GROWTH

Life is full of requirements. In order to do practically anything we need first to fulfill the initial requirements for doing it. Proper groundwork must be laid for any activity before it can be pursued.

Before we can start the day, we must first get out of bed. To enter an advanced course in astrophysics, we must first take basic courses in astronomy and physics. If we wish to raise healthy children, we would be wise first to develop a healthy marriage.

A strong structure has to rest on a stable foundation. So it is with spiritual growth; if we wish to grow spiritually, we must fulfill certain requirements before we can start.

Three fundamental requirements for spiritual growth are *desire, humility,* and *flexibility.* The recipe probably calls for other ingredients, but without these three, real progress is unlikely.

LIKE FUEL IN a rocket, *desire* is the driving force that moves us forward in spiritual growth. When friendship with God becomes important enough to us, we begin to work at it; we devote energy and attention to our spiritual lives. We must become hungry for truth. Our hunger for what is real and high must become piercing enough to poke through the humdrum pace of everyday living.

In order to move uphill, a buggy has to have a lively horse pulling it. In order to climb the rugged hills of spiritual living, our personalities must be pulled by a powerful desire to reach for the Father's Will. A weak wish that things get better won't suffice. The motivation to grow must be strong enough to break old habits. Then we can aggressively build new ways of living. We have to want God and growth enough to actually do something about it.

The Father wants to work with us. But He first must know that we want to work with Him. He will not force spiritual growth on us. If we want it, we must actively reach for it. He does not require sophisticated intellect, high social status, or even outward piety and virtue. But He does need our sincere desire.

If you are a poorly educated peasant with a fair share of vices but your sincere wish is to love God and do His Will, you will grow.

If you are a brilliant and wealthy doctor living a clean and respectable life but have little desire to search for the Father's inner leading, spiritually you will stagnate. It is largely your desire that determines how close you can eventually get to God.

THE SECOND REQUIREMENT for spiritual growth is *humility*. We must recognize our weaknesses, the areas of our lives where we have yet to grow. We must be humble enough to acknowledge that there are things wrong with us before we can go about correcting them.

We are not speaking of harsh self-criticism; self-dislike is undesirable. But if we are wrong in some way, honest self-appraisal is a necessary preface to improvement and growth. We must humbly recognize our imperfections while remaining optimistic about our ability to correct them.

Seen from the spiritual viewpoint, humility is in no way a weakness; it is a sign of strength. True humility is rooted in self-respect and faith. The spiritually humble person can look honestly at his weak points because he has faith in his ability to overcome them.

Being humble does not mean being passive and retiring. It means seeing ourselves clearly in order to act. Humility is the launching pad for aggressive growth.

FLEXIBILITY IS THE THIRD requirement for spiritual growth. In order to progress, we often have to give up old ways of living and explore new and unknown territory.

Human beings are creatures of habit; we often cling to what's familiar. We may sense that there is a better way to do something, but we stick to the less effective method simply because that is the way we have always done it in the past. Unfortunately, if we persist in such inflexibility we cannot grow.

Spiritual growth requires courage. It is not easy to be flexible, to leave the safety of old prejudices and familiar inadequacies in search of better ways of living. However, without such courageous flexibility, when the Spirit-guides present new truth for our consideration we will shut it out. New ideals will threaten us because they point out ways in which we must change. If we are afraid to change, we become inflexible and stop growing.

Flexibility is born of faith, assurance that the instability of new growth will give way to more stable times as we master our spiritual skills. At first, trying to live out new values is unsettling. But when we know that what we are doing is right, we learn eagerly and quickly. Before long, what was threateningly new starts to become as familiar and comfortable as our old ways used to be.

Then we can take a bit of a breather—at least until the Father's Spirit opens up new spiritual horizons before us. At that point, equipped with *desire, humility,* and *flexibility* we gather our energies and launch out farther in our journey of growth.

INNER AND OUTER GROWTH

In a sense, each of us lives in two worlds: one within us and one outside of us.

We each have an inner life where we experience thoughts and emotions, where ideals are born and grow, and where we can meet and communicate with God. It's like owning an inner mansion and having an honored houseguest; the Father has taken up residence within us. If we wish, we can have the privilege of spending time with Him, communing with Him, actively sharing with Him in our inner lives.

At the same time we also live and work in an outer world of human relationships and everyday activities. It is in the outer life that we encounter the stresses and strains of material living. How to find and hold a job, pay the bills, and get food and shelter, how to deal with a noisy neighbor and maintain sanity when the kids have been screaming all day long, how to tell your boss to stop harassing you—these are all challenges that confront us in the outer world.

One of the secrets of effective spiritual growth lies in harnessing the inspiration and energies of the inner life to transform, to uplift our actions in the outer life. Growth begins in the inner life, but to complete it we must translate it into outer living.

SPIRITUAL GROWTH HAPPENS in two stages: *understanding* and *becoming.* Both stages are necessary for complete growth. First we *understand* something new; we realize it in the inner life. But that is not enough. We must put that new insight into action in the outer life; we must actually *become* something new. Only then is the growth cycle complete.

As an example, let's take the idea that those people who are least able to be loving are the ones who most need to be loved. Suppose you have a clear inner understanding of this idea.

One day you are at work when a new employee comes on the job. He is particularly cold and distant and seems insecure. Despite your initial tendency to withdraw, and after some inner searching for the Father's guidance, you realize that this unloving person especially needs the love you can offer.

So you give him extra warmth and sensitivity and over the next several days he becomes more relaxed and friendly. He grows more able to love. Now you not only *understand* the principle inwardly; you have actually *become* the principle through your outer actions. By living it, you have made it real. The growth cycle is complete.

INNER AND OUTER GROWTH should complement each other. New ideals generated in our inner lives should inspire increased service activity in the outer world. Similarly, events in our outer lives should stimulate inner search and spiritual communion.

We need to strike a balance between inner and outer growth. We too often go to one extreme or the other.

For example, take the high-powered business executive, constantly on the go, meeting people, doing things, but devoting practically no time to the inward search for higher values and a relationship with God. His outer growth may be impressive, but his inner growth is practically nonexistent.

His personality is shallow: it is like a tiny box stuffed to bursting. His many experiences are crowded together within a cramped inner life. He needs to enlarge the capacity of his personality, to deepen and widen it through inner communion.

At the other extreme, observe the hermit monk who spends months in solitary inner search for God, but largely ignores the outer world of relationships and achievement. He may gain intense inner growth but his outer life is extremely limited.

His personality is like a huge box with just a few valuables rattling around inside of it. What a waste of spiritual capacity! Vast insight and understanding have little value unless something is done with them.

Such a recluse would do well to fill his enlarged personality with the treasures of service and love to other people. Then he would be approaching the ideal of spiritual growth: a personality that is inwardly deep and wide, and at the same time filled to overflowing with the treasures of outer accomplishment.

TO GROW HEALTHY and strong our bodies need two things: nourishing food and regular exercise. So it is with our personalities. To grow spiritually strong we need inner nourishment and outer activity. We are fed inwardly by communion with the Spirit. We develop our spiritual muscles by exercising them in outer service to our brothers and sisters in the Father's family.

Inner growth produces insight. Outer growth produces experience. When wedded together, insight and experience result in the essence of spiritual growth—wisdom. As such wisdom accumulates in our souls, our personalities grow.

HOW SPIRITUAL GROWTH HAPPENS

A common misconception in our culture is that growth and change belong to young people. The further past thirty we go, the more set in our ways we become. In reality, while we do stabilize in many ways as we age, we continue changing profoundly throughout our lives.

Each year brings broader challenges and deeper wisdom to those who are living in dynamic partnership with God. Even death itself, the end of the physical aging process, is but a passageway opening into vast new regions of growth. If we are reaching for perfection, spiritual growth is a process that never ends.

THERE IS A WARNING that usually applies to those who are just starting into the spiritual life: don't expect too much too fast. When we first begin to grow spiritually, there is often a transition period of some confusion and doubt. That is natural. It takes a while to grow fully into such a new way of living.

Picture a train five miles long starting up from a dead stop. The engine moves ahead immediately. But it may take quite a while for the movement to travel all the way along to the caboose. Similarly, the leading edge of our personalities may start forward in a spiritual direction. But it takes time and continuing effort to mobilize the rest of our lives to follow along.

When a child is first learning to walk, he often falters and falls. With continued efforts, though, he grows stronger and more skilled, and pretty soon his walking is measured and steady.

During the transition time which follows our first reaching for God, we are bound to feel somewhat shaky stepping into the newness of the spiritual life. Even so, we must keep on struggling to move ahead, reaching to build our connection with the Father's inner Presence. With time, our efforts will bring clearer and more powerful results. Our forward steps will become more consistent, stronger and more graceful. Our faltering first steps in the spiritual life will give way to steadier progress as we mature.

ONE TENDENCY THAT gravely threatens spiritual growth is impatience. It makes no sense to rush; there are no short cuts in the spiritual life. To go from lesson one to lesson five, skipping lessons two, three, and four in between is only to fool ourselves. Eventually we have to cover two, three, and four. A child does not grow by simply pretending to be an adult. He has to live day in and day out, year after year as a growing child, learning the lessons of childhood as he goes along.

So it is with spiritual growth. We cannot suddenly become full grown. We must go through a slow and thorough process of spiritual maturing. The heart of the process lies in all the tiny lessons learned along the way. Each ordinary day is filled with special riches.

The small decisions and actions of daily living form the real substance of spiritual development. Trying to bypass them out of impatience to reach the goal sabotages the very process of growth itself. It would be like throwing the engine out of your car to make it lighter so it could go faster. That would be senseless.

PERSISTENCE IS ANOTHER QUALITY that is most important to spiritual growth. We must pursue spiritual living with steady dedication. Occasionally, being human, we will slip up. But we should by no means get depressed and give up at such points.

By persisting, by renewing our spiritual efforts, we can again make steady progress in developing a strong relationship with the Father. Over a period of time, persistence brings tremendous results. In the spiritual life, a month of persistent daily effort is worth a lifetime of inconsistent attempts.

PERSISTENCE SHOULD BE balanced with the realization that we all reach plateaus in spiritual growth. There are periods when we are making strong progress, climbing steadily higher, working to explore and conquer new spiritual territory. But there are also times when we reach a plateau of growth, a place to stop and rest and look back at the ground we have covered.

At such plateaus we feel the satisfaction of accomplishment. We express worshipful thanks to the Father for His support and guidance along the way. Such plateaus of growth are times for spiritual refreshment. They prepare us to start out on new and more idealistic adventures.

Spiritual living is demanding. It takes lots of energy. Growth plateaus give us a time of spiritual recharging. In the relaxation of worship we can accumulate inner reserves, storing up a surplus of inspiration and motivation. Then we can return to the Godward climb with renewed vigor.

The duration of such plateaus of spiritual recharging varies. When we are moved by inner urges or outer pressures, they may only amount to short respites in the midst of continuing growth. Sometimes we can take longer stretches of such spiritual rest and relaxation before resuming the forward climb.

If we have been dealing with continuing stress and pressure it is especially important that we purposefully make room for such a spiritual "time out." We would not climb a twenty-thousand foot mountain without resting periodically to renew our energies. If we refused to rest, we would collapse along the way.

When climbing through difficult spiritual terrain, we should similarly make sure to pause for periods of worshipful rest and renewal. We should take time to refill our spiritual reservoirs with the inspiration that comes from deep communion with the inner Spirit. Spiritual growth must be balanced by spiritual restoration.

SPIRITUAL GROWTH IS POSITIVE; it is always far more effective to reach for what is good than to try to push away what is bad. Trying to *stop being selfish* doesn't work well; trying to *act generously* will be much more effective. Concentrating on *not screaming* at your child won't work; concentrating on *being patient and firm* with your child will result in the desired change.

It is difficult to overestimate the power of this principle. Spiritual growth is rarely a rejecting of negatives; it should rather be a reaching for positives. When we apply this principle, our growth efforts become much more fruitful.

Unfortunately, for many people religion means a constant suppression of wrongdoing, an everyday battle against evil. What a wearing and dreary way to live! The inner motivation of the person who is spiritually positive is quite different. He experiences a deep love for what is right, and delights in the spiritual life. Loving God and people is his greatest joy. Rather than a negative battle, spiritual growth is a positive privilege.

This realization that spiritual growth is essentially positive ties in with how we each use our will. It does not make sense to spend lots of energy fighting our negative patterns. By focusing on trying to squash our lower tendencies, we end up devoting more and more energy to these negative parts of ourselves. We cannot forcefully push out bad habits by sheer will power.

Rather than suppressing what is low, we should willfully direct ourselves to reaching for what is high. Do positive things. Develop desirable habits. Work for higher ideals.

If we cultivate such better ways of living, pretty soon these new habits will begin to crowd out the old and negative patterns. If we don't pay much attention to our fears but instead focus on living with faith and courage, before long our fears begin to fade, and faith and courage grow strong.

Our power to encourage our own positive growth is beautifully illustrated by the story of an old Indian chief. He is sitting by a crackling fire on a chill winter's night sharing his wisdom with the young braves of the village. He tells them of two dogs battling inside him; a mean, snarling, evil-tempered dog and a courageous, loyal, affectionate dog. They are fighting to the death, and whichever one wins will reign in the heart of the chief.

One young brave, unable to contain himself any longer, bursts out, "Tell us, please, Old Chief, which dog will win?" The wise man pauses, stares first into the fire and then into the face of the young brave, and replies, "The one that I feed."

THE PERSON WHO IS spiritually growing has something in common with the scientist; he is an experimenter. He is constantly upstepping his ideals and trying them out in the arena of daily life. He gets an idea on how to correct a shortcoming and he tries it out. He evaluates and learns from the experience. In this way, he finds out what works and doesn't work in reality. By experimenting, he learns how to apply his ideals practically, and thus he grows.

UNFORTUNATELY, MANY PEOPLE see spiritual growth as only one area of concern among many in their lives. Often it isn't even a terribly important concern. They fail to realize that spiritual values should actually pervade *all* areas of their lives.

Family life, profession, recreation, and education are all important. But it is precisely because they are so important that we should filter spiritual growth throughout these varied life activities. To think that we are too busy being parents, workers, and socializers to expend our energies on spiritual growth is self-defeating.

It is *only* by growing spiritually that we can fulfill our full potentials in any life-role. To grow spiritually *is* to grow in every other way. To ignore spiritual growth is to limit true development in all areas of life.

THE LAST POINT to be made in this section on the process of spiritual growth is that it is important that we stay fairly unconcerned about the process itself. Given our sincere desire to find truth, spiritual growth occurs spontaneously. We do not have to design and build it as we would a machine; it rather springs naturally like a plant from a seed.

If you place a seed in good soil and provide it with water, fresh air, and sunshine, it has within it everything it needs to grow into a healthy and strong plant. If you try to tug on the leaves to make them grow more quickly, or you wrench the plant out of the earth every couple of days to see if the roots are growing, it won't do very well.

A human personality grows in much the same way as does a plant. If it is watered by love and high ideals, if it is rooted in a desire to find God, then it has within it everything it needs to grow spiritually healthy and strong. Just as the Father has created plants with the inbuilt tendency to grow, He has threaded the spiritual growth urge into the very fiber of our personalities. Unless we somehow block it, it occurs naturally.

It is counter-productive to try to make ourselves grow faster, or to try to analyze ourselves so closely that we block the spontaneity of the growth process. Like plants, if we simply concentrate on reaching our roots deep into reality and turning our hearts upward in faith toward the Father's light, we will in the fullness of time grow most beautiful and strong.

Paradoxically, by concentrating on ourselves and on our own growth we actually block the ongoing growth process. We become so concerned with *our* betterment, *our* progress, that we no longer direct ourselves upward to God and outward to our fellows. Real spiritual growth occurs when we forget ourselves and love God—do His Will—and love people—live a life of service.

THE KEY ROLE OF IDEALS

People who build bonfires know that they burn best when wood is placed at the top of the fire. The flames can then reach upward, growing longer and brighter as they lick at the upper logs. As long as new wood is continuously placed on the top, the fire will burn high and strong. If no wood is placed on top, the flames recede and the fire eventually sputters and dies.

In order for our human personalities to grow continuously stronger and brighter we must be reaching toward higher ideals. Ideals are the stimulating goals that fuel the inner life. They draw us powerfully upward, challenging us to stretch, to grasp for the highest we know.

Ideals are guiding beacons which shine out from the Father's inner Spirit. In reaching for them, we strive to actually live out our highest conceptions of truth, beauty, and goodness.

Without ideals the fires of our personalities burn low. Growth slows to a halt; our souls flicker and fade. Life loses its purpose and we become listless.

When we look for and find higher ideals, we are motivated to live energetically. We are enthusiastic as we grow in pursuit of those ideals. We move ahead with zest toward each new inner goal. Our personalities become highly active, burning bright and strong in constant upward growth.

PERHAPS THE GREATEST challenge of having inner ideals is applying them to an outer world that is much less than ideal. It is rare that we can live out our ideals in the pure and perfect way we envision them. We must try to live idealistically in what is often a ruthlessly practical world. We must learn to translate our ideals into actions within the demanding arena of daily living.

Making our ideals practical does not mean compromising them. It means channeling them into real-life applications that will have a spiritual impact on the events and relationships of our outer lives.

A word of caution about ideals: there is always a sizeable gap between our ideals and our ability to live up to them. This is to be expected. Inner ideals have no practical boundaries; they can quickly climb as high as our imaginations will allow. To live an ideal in the outer life, however, we must put it into actual practice one experience at a time. That is a slow and applied process.

To be loving to all mankind is a wonderful ideal, and we can easily have such an inner ideal right now. To be loving to Harry next door, and the bus driver, and the lady that just backed into your car—that takes ongoing dedication.

Trying to catch up to our ideals is like racing against someone on a bicycle when we can only hop along on one foot. Our inner ideals are always racing way out ahead, and our ability to live up to them slowly follows along behind.

In fact, it often looks like our ideals are getting farther and farther ahead of us all the time. That might be a bit discouraging until we realize that the widening gap is a natural result of how ideals progress differently in our inner and outer lives.

WE ARE INDEED growing toward our ideals. But just as it is difficult to see the hour hand of a clock move, it is difficult for us to see our own growth as it happens. Our progress becomes much more apparent when we look back over a year or two and compare where we were then to where we are now. It is true that during that time our ideals have jumped way out ahead. But it is also true that at the same time we have actually made progress in our attempts to reach them.

THE PURPOSE OF INNER CONFLICT

Conflict plays a crucial role in our inner lives. It sets the stage for new growth. Rarely does growth occur without some degree of inner conflict. Conflict often arises when we first glimpse a new ideal, something higher to reach for. We feel tension because we are not presently living up to this new ideal. We recognize the gap between what we are and what we should be, and part of us wants to bridge the gap. But then a more backward part of us doesn't want to struggle to bridge the gap. So we experience inner conflict about what we should do.

One of three things can happen when we feel such inner conflict. We can decide to reach for the new ideal. We can decide to let go of the new ideal. Or we can postpone deciding and keep feeling the inner conflict.

IF WE DECIDE TO TRY to reach for the new ideal, the conflict is resolved. It's as if we are holding a bow and arrow, stretching the cord back to its limit, our arms quivering with the tension, and suddenly we release the arrow in forward flight. The impasse of inner conflict is broken. We free ourselves to move swiftly forward in new growth. The accumulated tension of the inner conflict is released in reaching for the new ideal.

We feel a sense of exhilaration when we thus liberate ourselves from our own indecision, mobilize ourselves to work in yet another way with the Father's inner Spirit. Such a resolution of inner conflict leads to increased spiritual growth.

IF, HOWEVER, WE DECIDE it is too much trouble to pursue the new ideal, we let go of it. It's as if we stop pulling the cord on our bow, relax our arms and drop the arrow to the ground. Once again the inner conflict is resolved. The tension is gone. But we have paid a heavy price. We have achieved a superficial relaxation of tension, but we have done it by killing the growth urge.

While such a decision may bring temporary relief from inner conflict, it cannot lead to real satisfaction. Giving up our ideals results in our losing self-respect. If a person gets into the habit of resolving inner conflicts by forfeiting his ideals, he is heading down a dead end street, fleeing from higher reality.

If he continues along such a course, the growing edges of his personality begin to shut down. Eventually his whole personality becomes inert.

It's true that when a person totally gives up his ideals he no longer experiences any conflict. But that is because in a spiritual sense he is no longer really alive.

THERE IS A THIRD RESPONSE we can have to inner conflict. We can just put off doing anything about it at all. That's like holding our bow and arrow at full stretch for an extended period of time without either releasing the arrow or relaxing our arms. Eventually the strain overcomes us and we collapse in exhaustion.

When we are thus frozen in inner conflict, we keep feeling the urge to release ourselves and grow but we keep holding back out of fear or inertia. Our inner tension continues to build as long as the conflict remains unresolved.

Such a postponing of conflict resolution is very destructive to our personalities; and it is more destructive the longer it continues. If we persist in not addressing the problem we begin to feel increasing stress. We lose self-respect and eventually collapse into depression. By this time we may even have largely suppressed the original inner conflict, but we are certainly aware that we feel badly about ourselves.

We can usually find the source of the conflict if we take the time to search inwardly. We've probably been avoiding an ideal that we know we should be addressing. To reduce the tension we must resolve the inner conflict. Either we decide to reach for the ideal, or we decide to let it go. Either we release ourselves and grow, or we give up.

INNER CONFLICT IS LIKE a person sitting in the driver's seat of a car and pressing on the gas and the brake at the same time. The car is fighting itself. If the person keeps both pedals pressed down, the car eventually starts to shake itself apart under the strain.

If he lifts one foot off the gas pedal and leaves the other on the brake, the car settles down. But he might as well turn off the engine because the car obviously isn't going anywhere.

If, however, he lets go of the brake and continues pressing on the gas, the car will move powerfully forward and cover new ground.

Spiritual growth occurs when we resolve inner conflicts by letting go of our fears and reaching for our ideals.

UNFORTUNATELY, MOST PEOPLE don't realize how crucial conflict is to growth. If we were always satisfied with where we were and never felt the inner tension of wanting to be somewhere higher, we would never grow. Conflict acts as a spur to progress.

Inner conflict is not pleasant while we are experiencing it. But it does pressure us to make choices, and thus results in the growth of our personalities. Often the greatest growth follows on the heels of the most intense inner struggle.

Our attitude toward conflict can directly affect our ability to resolve it. If we are afraid of conflict and avoid it, we will feel constant frustration in the growth process.

If, however, we see inner conflict as a natural part of living, we can approach it with optimism and assurance. We realize that conflict leads to growth. We recognize it as a positive sign that we are on the verge of new discoveries and accomplishments. If this is our attitude, then we will approach the conflict resolution process eagerly, and will reach up to embrace newly appearing ideals with enthusiasm.

THE WORK OF the Father's inner Spirit is not to make life easy and conflict-free for us. Rather, by presenting challenging new ideals these perfect Guides try to stimulate choices which will result in our growth. We feel conflict only as long as we delay in deciding whether to follow their higher leading.

The inner Spirit-guides constantly attempt to show us the deeper values underlying the conflicts we experience. By seeking their inspiration we can actually learn to approach conflicts with enthusiasm. For we begin to realize that each inner conflict, even though it may be difficult at the time, is in reality a gateway opening out into new realms of spiritual adventure. In time, we can even develop the habit of approaching such gateways of conflict with excitement, in anticipation of the growth rewards that lie beyond.

USING PROBLEMS AS OPPORTUNITIES

People often have the same negative attitude toward problems in their outer lives as they do toward conflicts in their inner lives. They see life-problems as a burden and they wish such problems would simply disappear. They fail to understand that each problem is in reality an opportunity for growth. In fact, without problems life would quickly become quite boring.

What we often fail to realize is that some of the things we enjoy most are problems. Planning how to get from one breathtaking spot to another on our Hawaiian vacation is a problem. Getting a golf ball into a little hole three hundred yards away, deciding which of three great movies to see, getting the right angle for a beautiful photograph, these are all problems. But we certainly would not wish to give up such problems.

Problem solving can be a delightful activity. It all depends on how we approach it. What makes a problem either a stimulating challenge or a threat to be avoided is largely the attitude we have toward it.

If we see problems as frustrating blocks that hem us in and ruin us, our stomach gets upset each time one appears. But if we can learn to approach problems on a higher level, to treat them as growth challenges that provide us opportunities for personal progress, we can begin to relate to them with openness and even excitement.

The key to feeling good about problems lies in gaining a spiritual perspective on them. It is important to remember that the overall purpose of life is to grow in partnership with God. Life problems are simply exercises in pursuit of that overall purpose.

It's similar to when we were learning to write back in grade school. The teacher would assign writing exercises (write, "See Jane jump" five times). The immediate problem was to complete the exercise. But the overall goal was to learn the skill of writing.

In adult life the immediate problem may be making enough money to obtain food and shelter. But the higher goal is to develop such traits as stability and perseverance in working out that particular problem in partnership with the inner Spirit.

From a higher perspective, practical problems are simply means to the overall end of spiritual growth. In fact, life-problems are actually *necessary;* without them we could not grow. Just as a fish needs water through which to swim, we need problems through which to grow.

When we realize how essential problems are, we actually begin to anticipate them because we see them as worthwhile. We start to feel good about dealing with problems when they arise.

THERE ARE THREE stages we go through in solving a problem: understanding the nature of the problem; finding solutions to the problem; and putting the solutions into effect. When we solve problems spiritually, we seek the guidance of the inner Spirit in each one of these three stages.

IT IS IMPORTANT first to understand clearly what the problem is. We must face the fact that a problem exists, even though we may feel weak or afraid in the situation. We have to discipline ourselves not to hide from our own weaknesses when a problem arises, not to distort reality by pretending there's nothing wrong.

Rather than fleeing from the problem, we have to approach and honestly explore it. Only by courageously investigating the problem and our part in it, can we understand it sufficiently to really resolve it.

We can fully explore and understand a problem by communing inwardly with the Father's Spirit presence. When we open our hearts and minds and sincerely ask for insight into the deeper nature of a problem, the perfect Guide within each of us tries to communicate a true picture of our situation. The deeper levels of the problem unfold in response to such inner communion. We start to see the problem clearly.

ONCE WE HAVE faced the problem and have gained a deep understanding of its nature, we can begin to search for solutions. The best way to find comprehensive answers is to work in close inner partnership with the Father. We are looking for solutions that will address the problem on all its many different levels, solutions that will allow us to live out spiritual values.

We should focus on seeking the Father's Will with open hearts and minds. We want to resolve the problem in the way that He would have us resolve it. If we persist in communion with His inner Presence, we will slowly come to an understanding of that overall highest solution which we seek.

IN THE THIRD STAGE, after understanding the problem and finding solutions to it, we must resolve the problem by putting the solutions into effect. This is often difficult to do. It involves deliberately changing our actions and relationships in the outer life.

This third stage of acting out solutions is made much easier, though, when we have thoroughly completed the first two stages in cooperation with the inner Spirit. When we understand the problem in depth and we believe that our solutions are right, then we can act with strong conviction.

Acting out solutions should also be done in cooperation with the inner Spirit. When we know we are heading into the thick of a problem, we can pray for courage and awareness to act in the way we have decided we should. And right in the midst of the problem situation itself, we can seek strength from the Father. We can ask Him to support us in our intended improving of the situation. Even when we are face to face with difficulty, God's inner guidance is available to us, if only we will ask for it and open ourselves to receive it.

SOMETIMES PROBLEMS SEEM to surround and confuse us. There seems to be no way to get around them. We start feeling like the little white mouse in the scientist's maze, running around, bumping into walls, unable to find our way out. However, if we look at the maze from the top, as the scientist can, we quickly see the way out. The solution to the problem becomes obvious.

That is why communion with the inner Spirit is so important in solving the problems of everyday living. The inner Guide can see our problems from a higher vantage point. If we seek God's inspiration, we too can begin to see our problems from "on top."

SOMETIMES WE CAN get very wrapped up in our problems. Our worry and concern, our over-involvement with the problem make it seem much larger and more complex than it really is. That is because we are no longer dealing with a simple problem in our outer lives. We are also dealing with a tremendous load of anxiety about the problem which we have created inside of ourselves.

For example, some people become so paralyzed with fear when they have to go in for a job interview that they can hardly force themselves to apply in the first place. The major problem for them is not the interview itself; it's overcoming their inner fears.

Tensions like these, which we create in our inner lives, often amount to 90% of a problem. We become so bound up in our own anxiety that we cannot get enough distance from the problem to see it in proper perspective.

When we sense that we are thus overinvolved with a problem, the best thing to do is to put it aside completely for a while and give ourselves over to worshipful communion with the Father. It's like slipping into a warm and surrounding spiritual bath. We can relax completely, surrendering to the loving embrace of the inner Spirit.

The purpose of such communion is to bask in the Father's presence, to express our love for Him and receive the expression of His love for us. It is a total sharing of ourselves with God, in which we rise high above the level of everyday involvements.

We emerge from such worship-communion spiritually refreshed and return to daily life with renewed energy for dealing with its challenges. Our outlook is larger and we see more clearly.

We are looking at "the maze" from "on top." The inner anxieties and tensions have been washed away. We may be surprised to find that what seemed like a crisis before worship, hardly seems to be a problem at all after worship. Our problems have shrunk to their true size. Now that they are no longer inflated by fear, we can deal with them much more effectively.

It is important to remember that when we feel overwhelmed by problems we should *first* put them entirely aside and immerse ourselves in communion with the Father's Spirit. And then, charged with the power, clarity, and joy of such God-man contact, we can return to deal with life's problems wisely and in full cooperation with the guiding inner Spirit.

WILL: THE DETERMINER OF SPIRITUAL GROWTH

Man is a unique combination. On one level he is a physical animal and on another level a spiritually sensitive soul. Much of the struggle and inner conflict that we experience results from the tug-of-war within us between these two levels of human nature. As previously mentioned, however, it is the very struggle of bridging these polarities in human personality that results in spiritual progress. Only human will can balance and harmonize these divergent urges. And thus it is our human wills that determine the pace of our spiritual growth.

THE HUMAN BODY IS a biological organism with roots that thread back through millions of years of animal evolution. Man has many animal urges and instincts built into his bodily nature. This is good. He has long needed such urges to survive in a physical world.

The human body is a phenomenon of nature. Like water running downhill, it seeks the path of least resistance. It instinctively seeks the least stressful type of activity, the situation that provides the most security and ease for the least expenditure of energy.

The body naturally moves toward what feels good and avoids difficult or strenuous circumstances. By bodily standards, paradise is a dry cave, a warm fire, a full stomach, and a mate to snuggle with, and we should never have been foolish enough to venture beyond such idyllic surroundings.

But the leading of the Father's inner Spirit and the growth-urge of our souls will not allow us to remain for long within the sheltered but limiting cave of mere material comfort. The Spirit urges us to reach for higher values. The inner Guide constantly challenges us to explore and conquer new areas of reality.

As we follow the Father's leading we often find ourselves in circumstances that are highly demanding and physically less than comfortable. We are often spiritually led to act in ways that conflict with our ease-seeking physical instincts. In extreme circumstances, people will even sacrifice their physical lives in living out their spiritual ideals.

Physical urges and instincts are legitimate and purposeful. We are physical beings and we must maintain ourselves in a physical world. But self-maintenance is not enough. We must also move forward. We must adjust our physical instincts to the progressive leadings of the Spirit.

In this life there will often be conflict between the inherent tendencies of the physical nature and the higher leadings of the Spirit-guide. The will is the mediator between these two forces in our personalities. Using our wills, we can balance and combine the physical and spiritual urges within us. Over time, we can thus weave a tapestry of wisdom between the practical demands of daily living and the higher beckoning of the inner Spirit. As a result, our personalities grow spiritually.

WE DO NOT ALWAYS choose wisely. When we allow our lower instincts to dominate at the expense of the Spirit's leading, spiritual growth slows and personality deterioration can begin. Such lapses of the proper function of our wills happen in a mild way to most of us. The contest between the material and spiritual urges is an ongoing part of our lives. Most of us, at one time or another, slip into laziness, fear, anger, greed or others of the baser emotions. Such an occasional lapse of will control is almost inevitable, and it simply delays our growth until our deeper motivations put us back on the right track of seeking Spirit guidance.

Departure from Spirit guidance becomes more serious, however, when a person is more or less conscious that he is doing wrong but goes ahead and does it anyway. In this case, his will is more than simply slipping because of negligence. He consciously knows there is a higher alternative, but chooses to ignore it.

Having thus consciously chosen to let himself slip backward, he has a longer way to go in order to once more accept Spirit guidance. To some degree, he has consciously chosen to rebel against the Father's Will. Such a choice poses serious obstacles to spiritual growth.

A person can sink even deeper into rejection of inner Spirit leading. If he consistently rejects higher leading time after time, such continuous rejection eventually hardens into an overall personality attitude of antagonism toward God.

Having willfully developed such a rebellious attitude, he shuts down all channels of communion with his Spirit-guide and devotes his personality energies to a life of self-service. He increasingly caters to his own lower emotions and instincts and abandons higher ideals. His personality deteriorates farther and farther toward eventual oblivion.

IN SUMMARY, A PERSON can fail to live up to his spiritual responsibilities on three different levels. He can temporarily wander away from Spirit leading. He can consciously reject Spirit leading in a particular situation. And he can move himself along a course of continuous and long-term rebellion against Spirit leading. There is one common denominator shared by each of these three different levels of spiritual failure; to a lesser or greater degree, the person distances himself from the leading of the Father's inner Spirit.

The farther we depart from the leading of the inner Spirit, the more difficult it is for us to return to the paths of spiritual growth. However, if our wholehearted motivation becomes the doing of the Father's Will, we can return to partnership with God regardless of how far we may have wandered from the spiritual life in the past.

It may take us a while to begin making solid progress once more. We have to reverse our backward momentum before resuming substantial forward growth. But if we sincerely desire it, no previous human error can prevent our resuming growth toward God.

We control the destiny of our personalities. We have the power to determine whether we progress along the eternal adventure of finding God, or become increasingly isolated in a dead end search for self-gratification.

HOW CAN WE move ourselves through the process of spiritual growth? One way of understanding this process is to look at the growth cycle as having five stages: *insight, choice, decision, action,* and *habit formation.*

IN THE INITIAL STAGE, *insight,* we first realize that there is an issue or problem that we need to resolve. For example, if we are walking along the street and find a wallet with $100 in it lying on the sidewalk, we are faced with a problem to resolve—what to do with this wallet.

The first stage of growth then is *insight,* the recognition that a problem situation exists—a turning point, a branch in the road where we can either take the path of growth or the path of avoiding growth.

THE SECOND STAGE in the growth process is *choice.* Here we search for and weigh alternatives.

We can leave the wallet in the street. We can keep the money and return the wallet to the owner. We can return both the money and wallet to the owner. Several alternatives lie before us.

In the *choice* stage we look at the alternatives and choose the one we will pursue. Hopefully, we seek the guidance of the inner Spirit as to the highest choice to make. When we have chosen our course of action, we move on to the third stage of growth.

AFTER CHOICE MUST come *decision.* It is easy to skip this crucial stage in the growth process. Many people make a choice as to what is the right alternative but they avoid making a firm, clear *decision* to actually *do* it. It is fine to have chosen the return of the wallet and money as the highest alternative, but then we have to decide that we are actually going to carry through on that choice. Exercising our wills is crucial at this stage in growth.

HAVING DECIDED TO CARRY through on our choice, the next growth-stage is *action.* We implement the decision, make it real through action. We determine where the owner of the wallet lives, go there, knock on his door, and give him the wallet.

THE LAST STAGE in spiritual growth is *habit formation,* the repetition of higher choices, decisions, and actions so that they become natural responses on the part of the growing personality.

After we have followed through a number of times on decisions similar to returning the wallet, such honest reactions start to become habitual. When faced with a choice between honesty and dishonesty, we tend to decide and act automatically in an honest direction. We have trained ourselves to react honestly to that type of problem situation.

When honesty or any other virtue becomes habitual, we have reached a new and more powerful level of spiritual growth. We have progressed beyond a particular sequence of insight, choice, decision, and action. We have formed an ongoing spiritual habit. We will explore the nature and formation of spiritual habits more deeply in Chapter 12.

SPIRITUAL GROWTH toward God is the fundamental reason for our existence. Progress in partnership with the inner Spirit is the mighty river that flows through human life. All life's activities and relationships are tributaries feeding into this mighty river of Godward growth.

If we choose to travel along with this great spiritual current, we can move ever forward through this life and beyond, through universes of growth toward the Father-Creator of all. We are His children. He would have each of us come to know and love Him in fullness.

CHAPTER

11

Toward Real Religion*

TWO SIDES TO THE RELIGIOUS COIN

Religion is a most controversial subject. Its critics have described it as a major source of war and hatred between men, as a psychological crutch that encourages man to be weak and unrealistic about life, as a powerful but corrupt social institution that unjustly dominates peoples' lives, and as an outmoded relic, a superstitious leftover from pre-scientific times.

Religion's supporters, on the other hand, claim that it can bring happiness to the individual and peace among nations, that it is a guiding light in an unstable world, that life is empty without it, and that man's hopes for survival and progress depend on his accepting religious principles of living.

How is it that people can hold such opposite opinions on the single phenomenon of religion?

The answer comes with the realization that religion is not a single phenomenon. Actually, religion embraces two very different types

---

*Note: The terms "religion" and "religious" are used here to refer to the *social institutions* created by *groups* of like-minded believers. As used throughout this book, the term "spiritual" refers to the unique inner personal experience of an individual.

of phenomena that unfortunately have been given the same name. Both phenomena have been called "religion" when only one really deserves the name. One is *real* religion; the other is *unreal* religion. Religion's critics are justified; they are criticizing *unreal* religion. Those who praise religion are also justified; they are praising *real* religion.

Unreal religions are dominated by fear and superstition. They breed feelings of mistrust and suspicion toward those who are outside of the religion. They often lead to an unbalanced, extreme life style.

An unreal religion makes rigid, authoritarian demands upon its participants. It requires total loyalty toward the religious institution and its human leaders. The religion itself has been bent to serve the unhealthy weaknesses of its participants and the power hunger of its leaders. Their dedication goes first to the institution, and only secondarily to God.

Real religions are dominated by love and trust. While participants might disagree with those outside of their religion, they maintain an attitude of tolerance and respect toward others' beliefs. Real religion encourages a balanced and full life.

Real religion supports the unique spiritual experience of the individual believer. It encourages sharing of insights between people in all levels of the religious organization. Real religion acts as a vehicle for the service-expression of the higher urges of its participants. They are dedicated first to God and second to their particular religion.

EACH INSTITUTIONAL RELIGION lies somewhere along the real-unreal continuum. Some religions are quite real and worthwhile; others are distorted and destructive—unreal. And most lie in between the two extremes, combining various characteristics of both real and unreal religion.

To the extent that a religion is unreal, it weakens and bends the personalities of its participants and retards the progress of the society within which it exists. To the extent that a religion is real, it uplifts and ennobles the lives of its participants. It transforms their personalities in line with the leading of the inner Spirit. Real religion stabilizes and furthers the progress of the society within which it exists.

THE DIFFERENCE BETWEEN DEAD AND LIVING RELIGION

Religion is real when it is alive, when it is a spontaneous and growing experience. When it becomes merely an established institution, a series of doctrines, a schedule of rituals to be performed, then religion has died.

When religion involves simply going through the motions, when it requires only passive conforming on the part of the believer, then it is inert, dead. Dead religion is a fixed set of rules and formulas. Living religion is an ever-growing relationship with God.

RELIGION IS DYING or dead when it becomes overly *doctrinal, ritualistic,* and *secular.*

A RELIGION HAS BECOME overly *doctrinal* when it emphasizes an established and detailed code of beliefs that the participant must subscribe to. If the believer agrees to every detail of the doctrine, then he is a true member of the religion.

If he questions any detail of the doctrine, he is considered a heretic, an outcast from the religious community, and supposedly he is rejected by God. To be in good standing he must conform fully to the doctrine laid down by the institution's authorities.

Such doctrinal smothering kills the spontaneous growth of religion. The religious beliefs of the individual can no longer develop. Eventually they slip into the background of his life. They become routine and humdrum.

Like the buildings on the street where he lives, his religious beliefs become so familiar and accepted that he hardly notices them anymore. His beliefs may conform thoroughly with the doctrine set out by his religion, but he is a religionist in name only. He has left behind the living spiritual experience that lies at the core of real religion.

A RELIGION HAS BECOME overly *ritualistic* when it substitutes standardized rituals for a living relationship with God. The religion decrees that if a person goes through the right ceremony and repeats the established prayers then he has fulfilled the essential requirements set out by God. Living in conformity with the religion's established rituals becomes the priority of the spiritual life. Living in intimate cooperation with God is almost forgotten.

The danger of such an unreal emphasis on rituals is that it lulls the believer into thinking that if he performs all these required rituals he has done everything that God wants. Having checked off his list of required religious duties, he can forget about religion for a while and go back to the "more pressing" matters of everyday life. What his religion has not told him is that God cares little for the rituals. What the Father most desires is the dedicated and conscious companionship of His children. He is not much concerned with whether we maintain the ritualistic frills; He wants our deep and ongoing friendship.

A RELIGION HAS BECOME overly *secular* when its primary purpose is to preserve itself as an institution. Tremendous amounts of energy are devoted to the business of running such a large religious organization. Clergymen become more administrators than spiritual leaders. The pursuit of power and influence dominate in the "upper management" of the religion as they would in any large secular institution.

Such a secularized religion is so caught up with running itself that it largely ignores what should be the primary purpose of any religion: furthering the spiritual life of the individual believer.

IN SUMMARY THEN, a religion is dead insofar as it is burdened with rigid doctrines, buried in ritual, and diverted by secular pursuits. With the passive consent of their followers, the leaders of such a misguided religion, whether they realize it or not, are displacing God from the center of the religious life.

These leaders are assuming that the individual believer cannot be trusted to develop his own strong relationship with God. They are assuming that it is their mission and their right to dictate the way in which other people should approach God.

They place themselves and the religious institution at the center of the believer's religious life. They write the prayers, they set the rituals, they tell the people what God wants and expects. The only way that the individual believer can come to God is through them.

To the extent that the leaders of a religion thus place themselves as necessary middlemen between the individual believer and God, to that extent their religion is dead. To the extent that the believer has a direct relationship with God his religion is alive.

A LIVING RELIGION encourages spiritual activity in the lives of its believers. To be alive, religion must be applied to life. The believer adapts the principles of his religion in a flexible way to the demands of everyday living. He is involved in a process of working out life problems in cooperation with the inner Spirit. He is constantly making spiritual choices.

Living religion is not simply acceptance of the fact that God exists. It emphasizes actual experience of His presence. Would you be satisfied simply knowing that your child, or spouse, or best friend exists? No! You would want to experience their presence, communicate with them, love them, and be loved by them. Similarly, living religion goes beyond intellectual belief and institutional obligation; it encourages a life shared directly with God.

A living religion supports spiritual growth. The believer's assumption is that there will always be higher truths that remain to be discovered. He realizes that his present religious views, while of great worth, are neither final nor complete. He is not satisfied with a frozen set of doctrines. He is constantly adding new insights to his present understandings.

DEAD RELIGION is unreal; it is passive, conforming, sedimented, and dull. Living religion is real; it is creative, spontaneous, ever-changing, experimental, and original. Dead religion is complex and unimportant. Living religion is straightforward and essential; it is loving God and loving people.

WHY WE NEED RELIGIOUS INSTITUTIONS

While the core of real religion is the personal spiritual life of the individual, the social phenomenon of institutional religion has a number of important purposes.

For one thing, religious institutions serve to maintain the spiritual momentum gained by the efforts of past generations. Religions gather and preserve the wisdom of each generation, thereby enlarging the overall body of truth available to mankind. Without this safekeeping function of religion, we would today have very little of the thought of the spiritual geniuses of the past.

Institutional religions thus serve as a river bed through time. They carry the flow of mankind's spiritual development from the past, through the present, and on into the future.

WE ARE SOCIAL animals. We can never be satisfied keeping our inner spiritual lives to ourselves. We feel the deep need to share with others that which is most important to us. We naturally desire the company of people who feel the same inner longings that we feel. It is altogether natural that we should gather with such like-minded people for the purpose of sharing our greatest joys.

The core of healthy social religion is this warm sharing of personal spiritual experiences and insights between believers. This is the most important purpose served by institutional religion: the promotion of spiritual fellowship.

These are times of tremendous social flux. Our society is being pushed and pulled by rapid changes. Cultural values are undergoing frequent and radical transformations.

In the midst of such instability, real institutional religions provide a haven of continuity for the spiritually motivated individual. A community of like-minded idealists can be powerfully supportive as we try to live by higher values in our confusing and abrasive modern world.

By sharing mutual support and clarifying a common vision we can strengthen each other to meet the demands of living spiritually in what are often unspiritual surroundings. As we participate in a religious group, we are nourished by the love and ideals that the group lives out. Inspired internally in our relationship with God, and reinforced externally through spiritual sharing with our fellows, we are well equipped to apply our spiritual ideals to the challenges of everyday life.

In times of personal stress and confusion our religion can provide group wisdom, guidance, and support. When we face a problem and can consult others whose values we trust, we have a distinct advantage over the person who must solve his problems alone. In interaction with our fellow religionists we can form a broad perspective on a problem, combining the viewpoints of a number of trusted friends.

WHENEVER RELIGIONISTS FORM a social group, some amount of ritual, doctrine, and secular organization occur. This is inevitable. There has to be some standardization, some commonality in language and concept for individuals to function together effectively as a group.

Personal religion can become institutionalized and still remain *real* and *living* if it embodies the following characteristics:

> The doctrines and rituals of the religion must highlight the living spiritual relationship between the individual believer and God.

> The doctrines and rituals must be flexible and growing. They must be elastic enough to accomodate variations in individual spiritual experience.

> The primary energies of the organization should be devoted to spiritual sharing and support, rather than to the building and maintenance of the institution itself.

> While individuals within the religion may have special organizational functions, no individual should have *spiritual* authority or supervision over any other. Religionists should be able to share with and enrich each other as equals. The only spiritual authority in the believer's life should be God.

REAL RELIGION TRANSCENDS INSTITUTIONS

Real religion goes beyond the borders of any particular organized religion. Real religion is founded on the relationship between God and the individual believer. No one religion has a monopoly on that type of relationship.

There are believers in every religion who enjoy a relationship with God. These believers scattered throughout the different organized religions of the world make up the true brotherhood of practicing religionists. In fact, they have more in common with each other than any one of them has in common with the members of his particular religion who don't enjoy a living relationship with God.

All real religionists, regardless of their particular religion, have several goals in common. They have developed an active inner spiritual life. They pursue a relationship with God however they conceive of Him. They reach for higher values and attempt to live them out in their relationships with other people.

Real religionists look for higher guidance in the living of their lives. Their common goal is to find and know God and to do His Will by cooperating with the Spirit that indwells them. Despite differences in tradition, creed, ritual, and religious terminology, all real religionists have these goals in common.

THE VARIOUS ORGANIZED religions are simply sub-families within the Father's world-wide family. Each religion reflects the long-term attempts of a particular group of believers to relate to God. Over time, they have developed traditions and beliefs that are unique to their group.

Such culturally diverse approaches to God should never war with each other. It is not that one religion is right and the others are wrong. Each religion is special in its own way. Each religion could easily be improved by absorbing the finer points of any other religion.

The different families of religious believers should relate to each other with respect and mutual appreciation. They all share God as their common goal. Each in its own way tries to bring man closer to God.

The differences between religions are what make the religious heritage of our world great. Each religion is a showcase for one more way in which man and God relate. We should admire instead of attack the religious differences between us. The very diversity of our religious traditions, the cultural richness of our spiritual history, should be cause for celebration. After all, God is no respecter of religions; the Father loves each of His groups of children equally.

Unfortunately, many organized religions have erected barriers between people. They have promoted differences of ritual and doctrine at the expense of loving brotherhood. *Real* religion never commits such an error. *Real* religion builds bridges between people. It puts loving brotherhood first and rituals and doctrines second.

Real religion is based on personal spiritual experience. It transcends the social institutions of organized religion. Real religion looks for common goals and appreciates the diversity of different traditions. Real religion promotes loving cooperation between the different groups of believers in the Father's family.

DO SCIENCE AND RELIGION CONFLICT?

One of the common misconceptions of our times is that science and religion conflict. Real religion, however, can exist side by side with science in full harmony. Science and religion focus on two different realms of reality, both of which are entirely legitimate.

The scientist uses the techniques of experiment to explore the material universe of facts. The religionist uses the techniques of personal experience to explore the spiritual universe of values. Both types of pursuit are necessary and desirable.

The dedicated researcher investigating the mysteries of physical reality with his scientific method can also be a sincere spiritual explorer expanding the borders of his higher understanding by the method of inner search.

In fact, science and religion need each other. Religion needs science in order to stay grounded, to keep from becoming superstitious and fanatical. When we know something of how lightning works, we are less likely to assume that God uses it to strike us down when we misbehave.

Similarly, science needs religion to guide its application in wise ways, to anchor it within a larger framework of values. For instance, we have the scientific capability to keep an unconscious human being "alive" for years with sophisticated machinery. Whether or not we should do so is a spiritual rather than a scientific question.

The trouble starts when either science or religion invades the other's territory. When religion attempts to make authoritative statements about physical facts ("the earth is flat"; "the world was created in six days"), it is trespassing in the domain of science. When science attempts to invalidate spiritual realities ("scientific proof is the only method for determining what is real"; "values are only learned patterns of behavior"), it is trespassing in religion's territory. Only when science and religion respect each other's borders, does their natural compatibility come to the fore.

Real religion welcomes the clarifying rigor of scientific inquiry. Although they do it on different levels, science and religion both pursue reality (science seeking facts, religion seeking values). They complement each other. When combined, they lead to a balanced, integrated way of life.

Living spiritually is entirely compatible with a growing understanding of the physical facts and laws of the universe. The progress of science can never undermine the foundations of real religion—love of God and the pursuit of higher values.

REAL RELIGION EMPHASIZES the coordination of spiritual insight with both the material and intellectual levels of reality. It encourages us to incorporate science—the critical recognition of facts—into our worldview. It encourages us to pursue philosophy—intellectual reflection on meanings. And it encourages each of us to guide our lives by the spiritual values which arise in our relationship with God.

These three functions of our existence—material, intellectual, and spiritual—aid and balance each other. Unreal religion is threatened by the material and intellectual tendencies in man, and so it rejects them. Real religion accepts and incorporates them. Real religion validates all the different elements in our personalities and harmonizes them toward overall psychological health.

REAL RELIGION KEEPS EVOLVING

Real religion is always evolving. To remain living, a religion must progress; it must grow. As civilization changes, religion must adapt in order to remain effective as a guide to living.

If our religions are rooted back in the worldview of the fifteenth century, they cannot provide meaningful guidance for we who live in the twentieth century. We must have religions that speak to the needs of modern civilization with its advanced science, rapid pace, and sophisticated outlook on life.

In past times when society was more stable and slow-moving, autocratic forms of religion served fairly adequately. There was little change in peoples' lifestyles from generation to generation. Religion could remain static and inflexible and still manage to meet peoples' needs.

However, to be effective in today's fast-paced world, religion must be more flexible, adaptable to changing circumstances. It must also be relevant for many different kinds of people coming from a great variety of backgrounds.

Modern religion must highlight simple but far-reaching spiritual principles that people can actually apply in their daily lives. And it must build light and flexible institutional structures.

MANKIND'S CONCEPTS OF GOD are evolving. Our early ideas were vague and filled with fear and superstition. Over the centuries, as our understanding of the world around us grew, we no longer attributed every thunder-clap and crop failure to the anger of the gods.

In more recent times science has largely freed us from such primitive explanations for natural phenomena. Each step that we have taken away from the primitive concept of the God of human emotions and nature-control has been a step forward toward the real God of divine love and spiritual inspiration.

It is time that modern religion shed the leftovers of fear and superstition handed down by the religions of early times. Primitive concepts of a jealous and distant God are no longer appropriate. Modern man has a right to know God personally as a loving, compassionate, and perfect Father.

MODERN RELIGION IS EVOLVING. It must shift its focus from ritual and doctrine to the actual experience of spiritual living. It must give up the struggle of competing doctrines and search for the seminal truths that underlie the traditions of all the world's great religions. A mature religion must live comfortably alongside science and philosophy. It must be motivated by love and the search for higher values. And it must be based on the direct relationship between the individual believer and the inner Spirit presence of God.

THE PRIMARY ACTIVITIES of religion should be loving worship of God and loving service to man. When large numbers of people give themselves over wholeheartedly to these activities, our world will experience the golden age of humanity's flowering. We will live *first* as children together in the Father's universal family, and *second* as members of our particular races, nations, or religions. Indeed, that will be the age of *real* religion.

CHAPTER

12

The Practice of
Spiritual Living

SPIRITUAL NOURISHMENT

Would we go for a week without eating? Or a month, or two months? Of course not. We need food on a regular basis in order to stay healthy. Without it we lose energy, waste away and eventually die. The symptoms of malnutrition are painful and clear; we would be foolish to ignore them.

And yet many people suffer the even more serious symptoms of spiritual malnutrition without ever recognizing or addressing the problem. Just as we need physical food on a regular basis to sustain bodily energy, so we need regular spiritual nourishment to maintain spiritual vigor.

Without ongoing spiritual feeding our personalities become undernourished, depleted. We become emotionally unstable and extreme. We feel isolated, fearful, inadequate. Attitudes of intolerance and anger begin to appear, and we lose optimism and vitality. All these symptoms indicate that we are not getting enough spiritual nourishment.

We expend physical energy as our bodies move and function. We also use up spiritual energy in the process of daily living. At the end of a full day of relating to other people, trying to love, be tolerant, and live out higher values, our spiritual reserves are somewhat depleted. We need to recharge, to re-energize ourselves with spiritual inspiration and insight.

A hearty meal provides nutrients and energy for a physically active day. A quick snack once a week won't do. Likewise, a daily period of intimate communion with the Father provides us with tremendous spiritual strength and stamina to meet the challenges of modern living.

God is a boundless source of spiritual sustenance. In the depths of prayer and worship He renews our ideals. He helps us strengthen our resolve to do His Will. He provides us a surplus of understanding and fills our personality reservoirs with love.

After a refreshing session of communion with the Father we are powerfully reminded of the sustaining presence of His Spirit inside of us. Thus anchored, we can "re-contact" the inner Spirit at many points throughout our day, drawing on reserves of wisdom and self-mastery that far surpass our merely human resources.

If we thus regularly contact the Father, He can keep us in a continuous state of spiritual "overflowing." We are able to pour out excesses of love and encouragement to those around us. We can celebrate the feast of spiritual nourishment that the Father has provided for us by sharing it with others.

FOR MANY PEOPLE today, the priorities of life are in a sense upside down. The spiritual nourishment of communion is taken care of last, if at all, and everything else comes first. That is like deciding that we will work and play first, and only if there is any time left over will we eat. It cannot work that way indefinitely. Eventually we weaken and break down.

Spiritual nourishment should have priority in our lives. Regular communion with the Father has to be at the top of the list. Developing and maintaining our relationship with God is essential to strong living. We cannot allow that relationship to be crowded out of our day by other activities.

When our connection with the inner Spirit comes first, all the relationships and activities of our outer lives work out the way they should. When we discipline ourselves to partake regularly of spiritual nourishment, we begin to live highly effective, balanced, and loving lives.

PRAYER: TALKING THINGS OVER WITH GOD

The secret of an active and healthy spiritual life lies in developing the habit of being aware of God's presence. It is important for us to realize that at all times He is here with us, close by, even right inside us.

There is no better way to hold onto that realization than to carry on a conversation with His inner Presence. And that is what prayer should be: spontaneous conversation with God.

It's like having a constant close companion along wherever we go and being able to talk things over with him whenever we wish. After a while such ongoing prayer becomes a habit, and our days become filled with joyous awareness of and interaction with the Father.

IN ORDER TO BE effective, prayer must be a two-way communication. Unfortunately, many people have become accustomed to the idea of simply "saying their prayers." They simply express themselves to God, often by reciting an established prayer, and figure that is the end of the process.

But that is like calling your best friend on the phone, telling him what happened to you today, asking for his help, and hanging up before he has a chance to respond. That would not make sense. And it would make even less sense if you called him once a day or once a week, repeated exactly the same highly formal message as the last time you called, and hung up before he could respond. And yet that is exactly how many people pray.

In prayer, it is just as important to listen as it is to talk. After we have expressed ourselves to the Father and have asked for His guidance, we must allow for a time of inspiration, a time of being open and receptive to the response of the inner Spirit.

It is impossible for us to listen while we are talking. So after we have expressed ourselves to the Father, we must *stop* expressing ourselves for a time, so that we can open our minds and hearts to receive His guidance.

EFFECTIVE PRAYER requests not only wisdom to understand but strength to *act*. If we ask only to *know* what is right our prayers are empty. We must also ask to *do* what is right. We must pray to be changed, transformed in line with the Father's Will.

For instance, let's say one of our children is continuously throwing tantrums and we pray for help in dealing with the problem. We get insights on how to change our behavior toward the child. We must then pray for strength to put those insights into effect. We must actually change the way we are acting.

Prayer is meaningful only when we are dedicated to *acting* on the insights gained within such prayer. In order to be effective, prayer must result in decision-making and growth.

EFFECTIVE PRAYER MUST be based on living faith. Communion with God assumes to at least some degree that there is a God to commune with. Even the person who has doubts and prays for confirmation of God's presence in his life, even such a fledgling religionist has the faith-seed of hope. His very desire to know of God, the prayerful request itself, is the first tender extension of trust from the child to the Father.

God is waiting for just such a request to make Himself known. When we pray to know God, we open ourselves to the awareness that God is already present within us. Eventually, such newborn faith-awareness grows into total certainty that the Father is lovingly attentive to our prayers. We grow certain that He will respond to our requests in ways that are consistent with His perfect wisdom.

PRAYER IS HIGHLY EFFECTIVE IN improving human relationships. If we are having trouble getting along with another person, nothing will better equip us to improve that relationship than to pray about it.

We can pray for the welfare of the other person. By persistently praying for someone, we open ourselves to God's view of him. We slowly come to understand him and eventually to love him. And loving him, we begin to act differently toward him.

Thus prayer results in improving our end of the relationship, really the only part of the relationship over which we have direct control. As we change, however, the other person will change in response to us.

Even when only one person in a relationship prays for God's help, God has access to that relationship and it improves. When both people invite the Father's participation, profound changes can occur.

PERSONAL PRAYER IS an intimate activity. We should do it in privacy, in a place free from interruption. It requires our minds to be focused and receptive. Because communion with the inner Spirit is often a subtle process, it can be derailed by outer events.

Public social prayer is beneficial but has different goals than private personal prayer. It more serves the purpose of social spiritual sharing and unifying of a group of believers. Spontaneous personal prayer, on the other hand, allows us to express our deeper and more intimate sentiments to the Father. Public prayer should never be allowed to replace our personal prayer as the central forum of communication between ourselves and God.

MANY PEOPLE MAKE the mistake of trying to use prayer as a way of getting God to do things for them. We could probably spend a long time counting the number of prayer requests for new cars. What many people fail to realize is that prayer is really a way of finding out what God wants us to do for Him. Instead of trying to change or influence God in our direction, we should through prayer be trying to change ourselves in His direction.

The inner Spirit is constantly trying to reach our minds with spiritual truth. Sincere prayer digs a deeper and wider channel within us along which such inspiration can flow. Prayer opens us up; it enlarges our ability to receive truth.

By praying to do God's Will, we go through a crucial change; we make ourselves ready and eager to receive what the Father is at all times offering to us. His Spirit is there at the door of our minds gently knocking. In sincere prayer, we open the door and allow more of the Spirit's constant leading to reach us.

The major effect of prayer is on the person who prays. Prayer makes us more sensitive to spiritual guidance. It strengthens us to live out spiritual values. Continuing and determined prayer leads to the inner changes that prepare us to lead the kind of life we have prayed for.

PRAYER IS ONE of the most reliable and potent stimulators of spiritual growth. If we are feeling despondent, depressed, spiritually sluggish and non-growing, a deep prayer session will open up new vistas toward which we can move. Prayer generates sensitivity to ideals. It is a key ingredient in the spiritual life of a highly active, growing personality.

PRAYER DOES NOT take the problems out of life. However, it does provide us with powerful spiritual tools to overcome them. In fact, the person who has developed the habit of prayerful contact with the inner Spirit tends eagerly to take on challenging new problems in his environment.

Sincere prayer heightens our sense of obligation to attack the problems of our world courageously. Prayer increases human industry and ingenuity. It does not lighten our load. By strengthening us, prayer allows us the privilege of assuming ever greater responsibilities in the service of God and man.

EFFECTIVE PRAYER CANNOT be superficial or hypocritical. It must be the expression of our heartfelt spiritual desires. When our prayer requests are wholehearted, they come from deep enough within us to generate lasting self-transformations.

PERSISTENT PERSONAL PRAYER unifies personality. The parts of our personalities begin to pull together in a common spiritual direction. As a result of prayer, the often conflicting urges of body, mind, and soul are harmonized under the influence of the all-wise inner Spirit.

Similarly, group prayer unifies people on a social level. It brings them together in cooperation toward the achievement of common spiritual ideals.

PRAYER SHOULD BE natural. It should be our spontaneous and easy expression to God and a natural filtering of God's guidance into our minds. God does not require formal and stilted salutations. Prayer is not a complicated or specialized process. We should be comfortable, free, and creative in our dialogue with the Father.

No matter how we pray, the Father will understand the deeper meaning of our expression and will respond accordingly. We need not prepare a special approach to Him. All we have to do is relax and pray in a way that is natural for us. Put simply, prayer is talking things over with God.

WORSHIP: APEX OF THE SPIRITUAL LIFE

Prayer naturally culminates in worship. At first we start off in conversation-like prayer. As we pray, our sense of the Father's presence and love for us begins to grow and our prayer takes on an increasing tone of thanksgiving. Prayer turns into praise. When we realize all that God is and does for us, our gratitude naturally swells, and our prayer becomes more and more an expression of heartfelt appreciation.

As our soul-expression of thanks becomes full-bodied, it blossoms into loving worship, an unstinting flow of love from us to God. There is a natural progression from the prayer of request through the prayer of thanksgiving to the joyous heights of unreserved worship.

WORSHIP EXPRESSES THE essence of the God-man relationship. It is self-forgetting and total giving. As human children, we offer up our total, unutterable trust and faith to our perfect spiritual Father. With joy and gratitude we pour forth our love for God. We release our full adoration for the Creator.

We hold nothing back. We harbor no shadow of mistrust. We positively know that the Father is worthy to receive our total human adulation. With soulful abandon and exhausting our capacity to love, we express the full depth of our affection for the heavenly Father.

And amazingly enough, in the very midst of this total expression of our love for God, we most deeply experience God's love for us. For it is at the very heights of worship that we encounter the Father most fully.

In worship we have our keenest awareness of God's presence, and thus our most pointed appreciation of just how total and all-surrounding His affection for us is. The splendor of His love is soul-shaking. It pours forth to us from His inner Spirit presence. It emanates from the very center of our personalities.

How completely appropriate, that inherent in the experience of the most total love we can express, is the experience of receiving that most total love that the Father has for us.

Worship is the ultimate sharing of love between God and man. It is profoundly intimate and utterly fulfilling. Such an experience of worship is the apex, the crowning pinnacle of our spiritual lives.

THE URGE TO WORSHIP is one of our deepest impulses. The desire to surrender totally to adoration of someone higher than ourselves is embedded in human personality. An obvious example is the tendency of a young child to fully love and admire his parents.

In primitive man, the worship urge was mixed with awe of nature and fear of the unknown. Early men worshipped everything from rocks and plants to sky and sun. Only as knowledge has liberated us from ignorance and superstition have we raised our worship-aim toward the true God, the Father-center of all reality.

HOWEVER, IN MORE MODERN times man has too often made another type of mistake: that of worshipping his own human leaders, governments, and institutions. Dictators, movie stars, and wealth all have one thing in common—they have all been objects of misplaced worship.

When man worships persons and institutions which by their very nature do not deserve to be worshipped, he puts true spiritual living aside. When he gives total loyalty to that which is less than the highest, great destruction and sorrow eventually result.

But we are slowly evolving to the point where we worship that which truly deserves to be worshipped. God is the only Person who properly deserves to receive man's unreserved adoration.

WORSHIP HAS A TREMENDOUS influence on human personality. Its full transformative impact is quite beyond description. In worship we align ourselves with God. We are energized and inspired to live spiritually.

The flow of deep worship refreshes and nourishes the entire personality. The body is relaxed and revitalized. The mind is cleansed of destructive thoughts and feelings; tensions and fears seep away. And the soul is flushed with joy, flooded with spiritual illumination.

WORSHIP PLACES THE rest of life in perspective. Our daily problems and conflicts shrink to their true small size when placed beside the infinitely large reality of God. We see them as the temporary realities they really are. Problems are transient; they pass on. God and our relationship to Him are permanent and growing.

This perspective is vividly experienced in the depths of worship. After such worship we can return to the struggles of living with renewed courage and optimism, confident in our progress toward the ultimate purpose of finding and knowing God.

In the loving communion of worship, our petty angers, fears, and jealousies dissolve away to nothing. We see them as the shadows they actually are, skulking in the corners of our personalities. In worship, the love and presence of the Father shine so brightly as to effectively banish these shadows.

The worship experience does much to lessen the influence of such negative emotions even when we once again return to the rigors of daily life. We remember to recognize them as non-realities and they no longer move us as they once were able to.

IN WORSHIP WE find our true place in existence. We directly experience God and our relationship to Him and thus our proper relationship to all of reality. We sense how and where we fit into the grand scheme of things, the unique position we each hold in the universe.

In worship we experience what we most essentially are: inestimably valuable children of the heavenly Father. For in the heart of true worship is the deepest expression/experience of that Father-child relationship—the overflowing expression of our love for God and the overwhelming experience of His love for us.

BUILDING SPIRITUAL HABITS

The ability to learn complex habits is one of the greatest strengths of human personality. By simplifying the process of living, habits save us huge amounts of time and energy. Without the ability to learn positive habits, we would experience great difficulty surviving in today's complex and demanding world.

Imagine what it would be like if each time the telephone rang we had to remember consciously what the ring meant, consciously decide whether to get out of a comfortable chair to respond, and then deliberate over what to say after picking up the receiver. We would spend ten minutes simply answering the phone.

And what if we got into our cars and had to remember consciously how to start them, put them in gear, and steer them? And when the brake lights of the car in front of us came on, what if we spent a few minutes pondering the meaning of such an event and a few more minutes deciding how to respond to this curious phenomenon?

Fortunately, all of these activities and many thousands more in a typical day are habitual; we do them automatically. If they weren't, not only would we fall hopelessly far behind in our daily responsibilities, we probably would not survive long enough to be perturbed about it. Forming complex habits is one of our most crucial skills.

Mechanical habits such as those described above contribute vitally to the efficiency, the economy of our lives. Without them we would waste so much time in repetitive decisions that we would never make it out of the house. In fact, we would probably never have been efficient enough to build houses in the first place.

Man's entire development rests on the foundation of his ability to reduce previous advancements to habit, thus allowing him to concentrate consciously on making ever-new advances.

THIS SAME ECONOMIZING advantage of habit-formation works on the spiritual level of life as well. We can build spiritual habits. Such predispositions to act spiritually save us lots of time and energy.

For instance, let's return to the earlier-mentioned example of finding a wallet with money in it lying in the street. We might spend the next two days wrestling with ourselves about keeping or returning the money. We can expend a tremendous amount of spiritual energy on such value deliberations.

However, if over a period of time we have by our previous decisions developed a consistent habit of acting honestly, we might spend only a moment or two deliberating before we decided to return the wallet.

When you consider that we face many such value-choices in the course of a day, the great efficiency of living that results from the formation of spiritual habits becomes evident. Each time we make a certain type of spiritual decision habitual, we free ourselves to concentrate on new and more challenging spiritual choices.

For example, when we have developed honesty as a spiritual habit, we no longer have to devote large amounts of our energy to decisions between honesty and dishonesty. Acting honestly comes naturally. We are thus free to focus our attention on higher spiritual challenges.

With continued effort, all types of spiritual responses can eventually become habitual, thus freeing us to address ever higher challenges. The building of positive habits is a central element in spiritual growth.

A HABIT IS AN ingrained, fairly automatic pattern of behavior that we develop through repetition. Desirable habits can be consciously developed.

An important point to remember about the development of habits is that it requires large amounts of energy to get them started, but very little energy to maintain them once they are well established. Suppose we are trying to develop the habit of praying for guidance when confronted with a problem. At first, we have to choose, decide, and guide ourselves consciously to engage in that process. The more often we do it, however, the more familiar it becomes as a response to problems. After a while it evolves into a regular pattern. We don't struggle with whether or not to pray; we just go ahead and do it. It takes substantial awareness and will to initiate such a prayer habit. But once it is established, little time and effort are required to maintain it.

UNFORTUNATELY, THE SAME learning ability that allows us to form positive habits can result in our forming negative habits. Negative habits often develop more or less unconsciously. We have an urge and we follow through on it repeatedly without realizing that we are forming a bad habit. By the time we experience the negative results of the habit, it's already well formed.

It would save people a lot of frustration if they realized that the best way to get rid of a negative habit is to develop a positive habit to displace it. It is very difficult to change a negative habit simply by trying not to do it. The more we concentrate on not doing it, the larger the habit looms in our lives. In a sense, we feed the negative habit by concentrating on it so much, by giving it so much of our energy.

Instead, we should concentrate our energy on developing a new and desirable habit which is incompatible with the old and negative habit. As the new habit grows the old one weakens and fades away.

Instead of fighting the habit of impatience, develop the habit of patience. Displace the habit of depression with the habit of joy. Knock out habitual greed by growing the habit of generosity. Balance preoccupation with material things by establishing the habit of worshipful communion.

Battle confusion; habitually stay in touch with the Father's guiding Spirit. Counter the habit of anger with tendencies toward tolerance and understanding. Overcome suspicion with habitual trust and conquer the habit of despair with the ingrained response of faith.

SOMETIMES SPIRITUAL INSIGHT occurs suddenly. We experience a surge of realization and resolve, and act with unusual spiritual clarity and courage. Such single spiritual events can result in significant growth.

But well-developed personality patterns must evolve over a period of time. Stable habits of spiritual living grow as a result of our repeated decisions and actions.

When such habits become well established, they pervade our personalities. They are woven into the very fabric of our characters. They become the permanent possessions of our evolving souls. Sound habits of spiritual living are the very building blocks of a healthy and fulfilled personality.

VARIATIONS IN SPIRITUAL LIFE STYLE

There are as many different ways to live spiritually as there are different people in the world. Each of us has a spiritual life style which is influenced by many factors of inherited temperament and environmental surroundings.

Since the temperament and experience of each of us are utterly unique, our spiritual lives, which lie at the very core of our personalities, are equally unique. Each of us develops an individual, highly specialized relationship with the Father.

Despite the fact that the details of one person's spiritual life are different from those of another, both persons' experiences are valid. The essential truths that the inner Spirit is attempting to show to each individual are the same. The way that people interpret such truths will differ.

FOR INSTANCE, ONE person might have a highly emotional but creative temperament. His spiritual life would likely be turbulent and far-ranging. In dealing with life problems such as finding a job, he would probably go through intense struggles and swings of feeling and might end up doing something quite out of the ordinary.

The same temperamental tendencies would likely characterize the tone of his spiritual life. He might experience many crises, emotional upheavals, and internal struggles in his relationship with God.

Another person might have an unusually placid and stable temperament. His approach to job finding would be methodical and balanced and he would probably end up with a fairly conventional type of job which he would keep for many years.

His spiritual life would likewise be very steady and perhaps a bit plodding. His relationship with God would grow in a slow but stable progression, and his spiritual life would be quite consistent from one day to the next.

IN ADDITION TO INHERITED temperament, a person's environment can also have an impact on his spiritual life style. One person may have been born and reared in a tribe in the jungles of Borneo. His understanding of the universe would be somewhat limited, his intellect geared toward practical survival. His world would comprise a few square miles of jungle. His social contacts would be only with the few other people in his tribe.

His inner life would partake of these environmentally determined qualities. His relationship with God would be simple and the needs of physical survival would play a large part in the rituals of his spiritual life.

Another person may have grown up in a college community in a modern industrialized country, and may currently be a professor of the Psychology of Religion at Yale University. He might travel extensively, meeting different types of people from all around the world.

This person's concepts of the universe and reality would be broad. His spiritual life would probably be complex and well thought out, his experience with God many-faceted.

THE INDIVIDUALS DESCRIBED above exhibit variations in spiritual life style due to differences in temperament and environment. However, the most crucial factor that determines the quality of any person's inner spiritual life is neither hereditary nor environmental.

The quality of our spiritual lives depends fundamentally on our own will decisions and actions. If our desire to know God is strong and if we act on such motivations, no handicap of heredity or environment can block us from sharing our spiritual lives with the Father.

Such handicaps may temporarily delay our spiritual development. But eventually, in the fullness of eternity, our inner motivation will overcome all obstacles to a deep and satisfying relationship with God.

THE QUALITIES OF SPIRITUAL LIVING

One of the outstanding qualities of the spiritual life is *balance.* In a balanced personality, no one element dominates at the expense of the others. Too much of even a good thing is harmful. Each virtue that we develop should be balanced by other virtues that keep it from becoming extreme.

For example, if we are truly living spiritually, as we grow more powerful we at the same time grow more self-controlled. We are mightily moved by inner inspiration but maintain outward poise and social grace. We develop strong ideals and principles while respecting the viewpoints of others. We live boldly, courageously, but are not foolhardy or fanatical. We blend idealism and practicality.

We humbly accept our limitations but vigorously dedicate ourselves to the pursuit of higher goals. We feel and express strong emotions but we can redirect and transform them along lines of Spirit guidance. Our emotional lives are both deep and self-mastered.

Our outlook on life is a balance of mature adult wisdom and childlike trust. We combine seriousness with humor, work with play, and solitary contemplation with friendship relations. We are loving and considerate but do not accomodate weakness in others.

Achieving such balance of personality is indeed a long-term project. We evolve it through living experience as we seek and follow the leading of the Father's inner Spirit.

MANY PEOPLE MISTAKENLY assume that the goal of the spiritual life is to leave everyday reality behind. They claim it is unreal, an illusion. They reach for rarified states of consciousness, mystical visions that remove them from mundane existence. They want to elevate themselves to a supposedly more "real" level of awareness.

Contrary to such thinking, one of the finest qualities of the spiritual life is that it is practical; its medium is everyday life. The idea is not to escape material living, but rather to transform and uplift it through spiritual inspiration. As we live spiritually, we begin to mold and change our everyday lives, bringing them increasingly in line with the Father's Will.

ANOTHER MISTAKEN NOTION is that the main event in the spiritual life is an intense emotional experience that sweeps over us and then subsides. While it is true that strong emotions may accompany our inner spiritual experience, they are only the surface signs of value changes that happen much deeper in our personalities.

Long after the glow of such a high emotional moment has passed, the deeper spiritual values remain as transforming factors in our lives. The goal of spiritual living is not the attainment of peaks of emotional rapture, but rather the deep, broad, and long-term growth of personality in partnership with God.

ONE QUALITY THAT IS crucial to balanced spiritual living is humor. Unfortunately, people too often assume that religion is a somber, deadly serious pursuit, allowing for no humor or joy.

Nothing could be further from the truth. Spiritual living by and large is fun. Loving God and people is a most enjoyable activity. Real religion is totally compatible with hilarity.

Laughter is a great tonic for overall personality health. Humor keeps us from taking ourselves too seriously; it counters the build-up of dangerous levels of pride. Relaxed good times renew and lubricate our personalities, preparing us to take on new challenges in spiritual living.

THE PURSUIT OF PLEASURE is consistent with spiritual living so long as it remains in proper balance with all other parts of life. Unfortunately, modern society emphasizes self-gratification to an unhealthy degree. The entertainment/pleasure craze, the ravenous pursuit of self-pleasing distractions is inconsistent with spiritual living.

Two very important functions in the spiritual life are *setting priorities* and *maintaining simplicity*. In living spiritually, we decide which parts of life are more important than others and apportion our energies accordingly. We realize that there are thousands of activities and opportunities available in our complex world and that some are much more worthwhile than others.

We simplify our lives, devoting energy to those activities which fit our spiritual values and letting go of those activities which are relatively without value. We recognize that we must winnow out the useless complexities. We lessen our preoccupation with superficial pleasures. We increasingly turn to higher pleasures, to those activities which fill the deeper hungers of our souls. It's not that we pull out of everyday life. It's simply that we try to live within it more selectively.

The spiritually wise person distinguishes between *destructive* pleasures and *constructive* pleasures. Destructive pleasures are time-wasting, energy-depleting, and have no lasting value. They usually weaken and deteriorate all parts of our personalities. Getting drunk is a prime example of a destructive pleasure.

Constructive pleasures are healthful to our bodies, stimulating to our minds, and consistent with higher values. They renew energy and consolidate the worth of previous experiences. One of the most constructive forms of pleasurable recreation is relaxed fellowship with others who are spiritually motivated.

THE RESULTS OF SPIRITUAL living are quite obvious. We experience an unshakable sense of peace and optimism. We share our excess of love and joy with those around us. And we revel in the fulfillment of leading a life bursting with meaning and purpose.

It is said that if we spend enough time with a friend we begin to take on his qualities. It makes sense then, that as we spend time in friendship with the Father, His magnificent qualities begin to rub off on us. Slowly but surely His divine nature begins to pattern our spiritual living.

HIGHLIGHTS

This section highlights the central spiritual truths described in previous chapters.

THE FATHERHOOD OF GOD

God is first and foremost a loving, wise, and perfect parent to His spiritual children. Each one of us, as His growing spiritual child, enjoys the opportunity for a unique and deeply personal relationship with the Father. He is our source and destiny; we are of tremendous value to Him and He loves us infinitely.

What must we do to experience the ecstasy of being the Father's children? Simply have faith. With childlike trust we can open our hearts and minds to His Presence.

THE BROTHERHOOD OF MAN

We share God as our Father; thus, all people are in the deepest sense our spiritual brothers and sisters. We are each of us members in the worldwide family of God.

Since any other person is another of the Father's children, we should strive to give him the love and caring which the Father so generously gives to us. It is fitting that His love flow through us, outward in spiritual service to our brothers and sisters in His family.

GOD'S INDWELLING SPIRIT

God has given us the ultimate gift. He has sent an actual Spirit-fragment of Himself to dwell within our human minds. This devoted Spirit works patiently for our spiritual growth in this life and the next.

The Father is thus nearer to us than any other person. He knows us perfectly from within. We are not isolated in the universe; God is our constant inner companion. We can open our hearts and share our inner lives with the Father. The indescribable joys of deepening friendship with His indwelling Spirit are ours for the choosing.

THE WILL OF GOD

The Father has a unique Will for our lives, from our small daily actions to our largest life decisions. His Spirit presence constantly strives to show us the divine Will during each passing moment.

It is most important for us to first seek and then try to do the Father's Will. For it is by our decisions and actions that we grow spiritually. By praying persistently for guidance and strength to do God's Will, we can each develop an effective working partnership with His inner Presence. Real religion is more than a set of beliefs; it is an actual way of living with the guidance of God.

REACHING FOR HIGHER VALUES

The highest values for which man can reach are truth, beauty, and goodness. The expression of these values is best unified in spiritual love. Trying to bring these higher values into our everyday living is a powerful way to experience and express the love of the Father.

These supreme values are like three mighty rivers running to the ocean. Scientific and philosophic truth, aesthetic beauty, and spiritual goodness are all compatible; they each add to a fuller appreciation of the Father's infinite universe.

PERFECTION AS THE GOAL

The perfection of the Father is our goal. We begin the search here and follow it into eternity. It is in the difficult arena of everyday existence that we must strive for the highest way to live. The Father helps us in our struggle for perfection.

Our deepest desires and yearnings are what matter most to God. Our actual achievements and failures in reaching for perfection are secondary. The Father knows that if our intent is deep and true, eternity will afford us the opportunity to reach our goal.

AN ETERNAL LIFE OF GROWTH

Life is not a dead end street; death is but the doorway to an eternal existence. Our yearnings for exploration and adventure are not in vain. Stimulating challenges await us in an eternal ascent of struggle and growth toward God.

The exhilaration of masterful achievement through personally earned experience will characterize our path through eternity. And this never-ending life can begin for us now if only we will sincerely choose, with faith, to begin the eternal adventure of seeking and finding God.

TRY IT: YOU'LL LIKE IT!

All the ideas in this book are worthless if you the reader treat them simply as ideas. Ideas become real only as they are translated into the living reality of personal experience. Many books can be read, thought about, and shelved. To be valid, the ideas in this book must be read, thought about, and lived.

There is only one way to find out whether the ideas presented here are true. Experiment with them in your life. No person or book alone can prove them to you logically. Only *you* can conclusively prove the existence of God. The only person who can find Him in your inner life is *you.*

You stand at the doorway opening into the supreme adventure of time and eternity. It is your decision whether to enter. God Himself awaits your choice.

Go ahead! Try it: you'll like it!

IF YOU ENJOYED THIS BOOK . . .

. . . and would like to order additional copies

- for friends
- as gifts
- as a study group aid
- as a classroom text

*You can order copies through your local book store.

*You can obtain copies directly from the publisher by filling out and sending the order form below.

*Discounts available on quantity orders:

5 to 9 copies: 10% off	30 to 49 copies: 30% off
10 to 29 copies: 20% off	50 to 99 copies: 40% off

100 copies and up: 50% off

*Standard industry discounts to distributors and retailers.

- -

NAME_____

ADDRESS_____

CITY_____ STATE_____ ZIP_____

Please send me _____ copies of **Reaching High: The Psychology of Spiritual Living.**

____ copies softcover edition at $7.95 each (California residents please add 48¢ sales tax per copy).

____ copies hardcover edition at $11.95 each (California residents please add 72¢ sales tax per copy).

Please make checks or money orders payable to:

SPIRITUAL RENAISSANCE PRESS

315 Harvard Ln.
Boulder, CO
80302